THE LORDSHIP, PARISH AND BOROUGH

OF MONMOUTH

ALSO BY KEITH KISSACK

Mediaeval Monmouth, 1974
Monmouth: The Making of a County Town, Phillimore, 1975
Victorian Monmouth, 1977
The River Wye, Terence Dalton, 1978
The River Severn, Terence Dalton, 1982
Monmouth and its Buildings, 1991
Blue Guide to Churches and Chapels: Herefordshire, Shropshire and Worcestershire (with Adrian Barlow), 1991
Monmouth School and Monmouth 1614-1995, Lapridge, 1995

THE LORDSHIP, PARISH AND BOROUGH OF MONMOUTH

Keith Kissack

LAPRIDGE PUBLICATIONS
1996

First published in 1996 by
Lapridge Publications
25 Church Street
Hereford HR1 2LR

Some of the material herein first appeared in *Mediaeval Monmouth*
published in 1974 by The Monmouth Historical and Educational Trust

ISBN 1 899290 03 6

British Library Cataloguing in Publication Data.
A catalogue record for this book is available
from the British Library.

Printed in Great Britain by
Biddles Limited

To the Monmouth Archaeological Society
whose activities over the last forty years
provided the inspiration for
the publication of *Mediaeval Monmouth* (1974)
and have made necessary this much expanded new work

CONTENTS

KEY TO ABBREVIATIONS AT END OF EACH CHAPTER

CDF   *Calendar of Documents in France, 818-1200* by J.H. Round.
           (HMSO, 1899).
DL   Duchy of Lancaster.
EHR   English Historical Review.
JHSCW   Journal of the Historical Society of the Church in Wales.
LL   Liber Landavensis
MA   Monmouthshire Antiquary.
MBA   Monmouth Borough Archives in Monmouth Museum.
PM   *Presenting Monmouthshire*.
Regist   Hereford Cathedral Registers, 1275-1535.
SWMRS   South Wales and Monmouthshire Record Society.

FOREWORD
by
Sir Richard Hanbury-Tenison, KCVO
Lord Lieutenant of the County of Gwent

Monmouthshire (latterly Gwent) has been lucky in its historians: Williams in 1796, Archdeacon Coxe in 1801, Bradney between 1904 and 1929 and, in our own generation, Keith Kissack who has worked on the history of Monmouth for many years and has published a number of important and entertaining books on the town. The present work completes his *Monmouth: The Making of a County Town* (1975) which deals primarily with the eighteenth and nineteenth centuries. We now learn how the town developed from the coming of the Normans to the end of the seventeenth century, and it is a tribute to Keith Kissack's wide historical knowledge and his keen eye for a story that these early centuries produce almost as many memorable characters, and rather more villainous ones, than the better documented period of the earlier book. We now learn all there is to know about the building of the castle and the church and how the townspeople of those earlier centuries lived, what concerned them and sometimes how they died; all the more interesting in a town such as Monmouth where so much that our forebears knew has survived into our own day. Monmouth is a very special town and we can now read its history as never before.

Clytha Park
Summer 1996

PREFACE AND ACKNOWLEDGEMENTS

Mediaeval Monmouth was published in 1974 and has long been out of print. Since it was written the Monmouth Archaeological Society has produced much new information about the period that the book covered. So this book has taken a different format and covers a wider range of time and subject. I have tried to co-ordinate the new archaeological evidence with the existing documentation, but realise that while excavation continues this must provide an incomplete picture.

Wherever possible I have given the original references but, where they are missing, I have also used the ten volumes of transcriptions J. Hobson Matthews made in 1908 for the Mayor of Monmouth, the Honourable J. M. Rolls. Hobson Matthews had been Cardiff City archivist and the editor of *Cardiff Records*. He was asked to make this report on all known Monmouth records after it became known that the landlord of the Nag's Head Inn had found a large collection of old papers in his attic and, because he could not understand the language, made a bonfire of them. So perished many of Monmouth's earliest documents.

I am indebted to many people, especially Stephen Clarke and the members of the Monmouth Archaeological Society for information and financial assistance; to Sir Richard Hanbury-Tenison for writing the foreword; to Lyn Harper and Andy Smith for their meticulous plans; to Owen Morgan and M. P. Watkins for information about the river; to Derek Jones, Craig Relyea and Fr. David Smith for photographs; to Kirstie Buckland; to the curator and staff of the Monmouth Museum; to the Welsh Church Fund for a grant towards publication; and to many individuals whose advice I have sought. Not least of these has been Paul Latcham who has gracefully guided a difficult script through the dreaded stages of publication. As usual the chief sufferer has been my wife and to her I am eternally grateful.

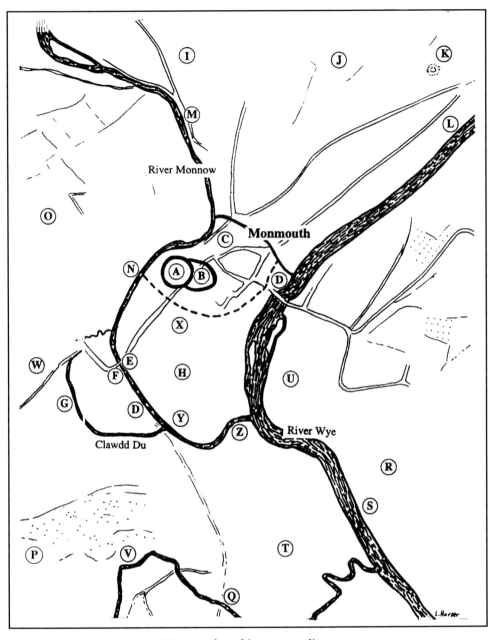

Monmouth and its surroundings

A	Castle and Inner Bailey	N	Castle Mill
B	Outer Bailey and Barton	O	Castle field
C	Benedictine Priory	P	St. Duellus (St. Dials)
D	Wharves	Q	Trothy Bridge
E	Monnow Bridge	R	St. Thomas, Wyesham
F	St. Thomas, Overmonnow	S	Hall of Lord of Wyesham
G	Clawdd Du Bridge	T	Warretreham
H	Chippenham	U	Selnorsmede (later The Soldiers' Meadow)
I	The Vineyard ?	V	Holywell Wood
J	Dixton field	W	Williamsfield
K	Hall of the Lord of Dixton	X	Butt Acre
L	Dixton Church	Y	Goose Acre
M	Monnow Mill	Z	Old course of the River Monnow

INTRODUCTION

Below the late fifteenth century oriel on Monmouth's Benedictine priory, are three carved heads; a knight, an angel and a miller. They represent three of the elements on which the prosperity of this small mediaeval community depended. The knight from his castle ruled a lordship which provided security, justice and the land on which all depended. The angel, bearing the arms of England, through the priory and eventually the parish, provided the means of spiritual salvation. The miller, through the market, the burgesses and the borough, provided the creature comforts of everyday life. There were later elements peculiar to a county town, which Monmouth was to become; the assizes, the militia, the schools, each of which can be placed conveniently under one of the heads. These three symbolic heads have roughly dictated the sequence of this book.

This was not, of course, the beginning of Monmouth. Palaeolithic and Mesolithic travellers left evidence of their passage here and in the neighbouring Doward hills and caves[1], while Iron Age immigrants probably built the impressive hill fort on the adjoining Little Doward. It covers nineteen acres, is defined by single and multiple ramparts, and is the most impressive fortification in the Monmouth area. Its occupants may well have combined with native Bronze Age people who had settled in Monmouth to defend their territory against the next wave of invaders from Europe, the Romans.[2]

The Antonine Itinerary of the early third century AD refers to Monmouth as Blestium. The site seems to have been chosen because of its proximity to the iron ore of the Forest of Dean and the convenience of the river crossings. From this mixed industrial and military centre a web of roads spread out; north-west to Ariconium (near Ross) and Glevum (Gloucester), north to Magna (Kenchester), west to Gobannium (Abergavenny), south-west to Burrium (Usk) and Isca (Caerleon), and south to Venta (Caerwent). Coins found in the town date mainly from the end of the third century to the middle of the fourth. Recent excavations by the Monmouth Archaeological Society indicate that Blestium covered an area of flood-free ground between the Wye and the Monnow and beyond.[3]

Further excavations by that society have revealed an extensive layer of plough soil separating the traces of the Roman occupation from the arrival of the Normans. From that long interval in time, elements of the post-Roman

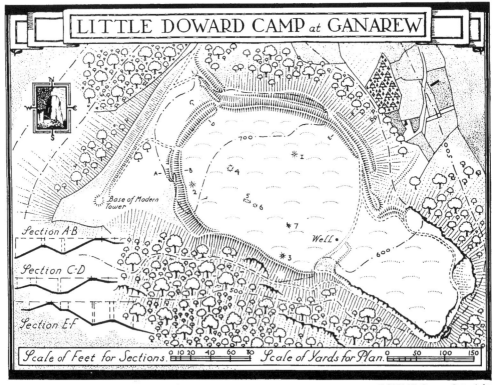

Iron Age fort on Little Doward.

occupation survived on the banks of the Wye. There was a Celtic church dedicated to St. Cadoc near the site of the future castle. The Great Causey, later to become Monnow Street, was an ancient trade route to the west. A mile up the Wye was the Celtic church of Llan Tydwg (Dixton) facing across the river the Saxon settlement of Hodenac (Hadnock).

Evidence for the existence of Dixton in the eighth century depends on the Llandaff charters, one of which refers to a grant by King Ithel of 'a podium [an ecclesiastical community] called Henlann Tydiuc with four modii of land around it [c. 160 acres] and its weirs to Bishop Berthgwyn for the soul of his son Arthrwys'.[4]

Over three hundred years later another charter records that, 'before the castle of Mingui [Monmouth] was built, Bishop Herwald consecrated Llan Tidiuc and ordained Ris as priest, and he dying ordained his sons, Guriul and Duinerth'.[5] That reconsecration may have been caused through the destruction of the church by raiders heading upstream to Hereford in 1056.

As yet not fully explained was a massive wooden structure, its foundations excavated by the Monmouth Archaeological Society. It stood on huge timber posts in the middle of Monmouth on the Great Causey close to St. Cadoc's church. Being to the west of the Wye it was presumably Celtic, but there is a possibility that Saxon intruders from Hadnock built it to safeguard trade

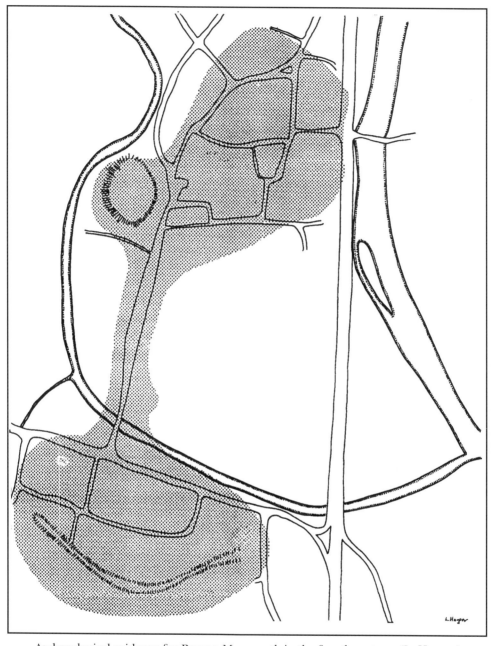

Archaeological evidence for Roman Monmouth in the fourth century. (L. Harper)

from the Forest of Dean.[6]

More definite evidence for pre-Conquest life in this area is a hoard of coins of Aethelred II, possibly looted, found on a hillside overlooking Monmouth in 1991. It consisted of eleven silver pennies and a cut halfpenny dating from AD 991 to 997.[7]

Moreover Monmouth lay at the southern tip of Archenfield, a small independent Welsh community known to the Saxons as the Dunsaete (the hill

15

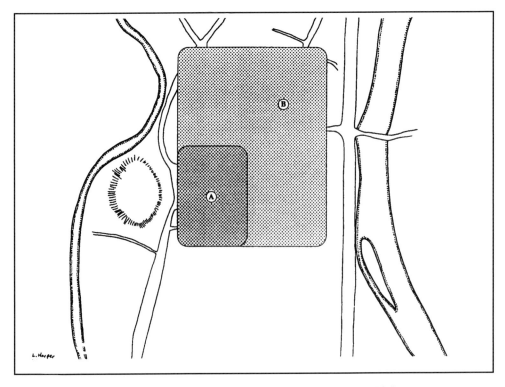

A   Probable position of pre-Flavian auxiliary Roman fort (mid first century).

B   Possible position of vexillation fort.

folk). Their pre-Conquest customs are meticulously recorded in the Domesday Survey. Monmouth's position there, on a rich flood plain between easily-crossed rivers, linked two widely differing regions, the Forest of Dean to the east, and Celtic Wales to the west.

REFERENCES Introduction

    (Abbreviations for some of the more frequently cited sources appear on page 8)

[1]   S. Clarke, *The Stone Age around Monmouth*, 1984.

[2]   S. Clarke, *Early Iron Working around Monmouth*, 1981.

[3]   A.L. Sockett, *The Monmouth District in Antiquity*, 1960.

[4]   LL (Edition Evans), p.183.

[5]   Ibid., p.276.

[6]   S. Clarke, '22-24 Monnow Street', 1991 and 'Evidence for a Pre-Norman Structure at Monmouth'.

[7]   S. Clarke, 'The Monmouth Hoard of Aethelred II Coins' in *The Monmouthshire Antiquary*, XI (1995), p.55.

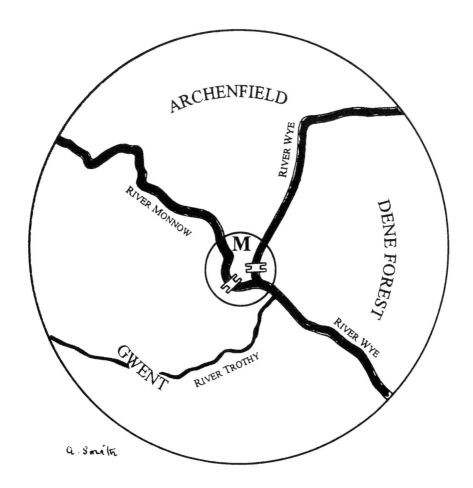

The position of Monmouth.

Part One
THE BRETON LORDS 1067-1256

1 The Lordship

 Shortly after Hastings the pacification of the southern Welsh border was entrusted to a cousin of the Conqueror, William FitzOsbern, Seneschal of Normandy. Created Earl of Hereford for the purpose, he quickly subdued Archenfield and before his death in 1071 had established, near the confluence of the Wye and the Monnow, the Castle of Monmouth. At this early stage, with its timber building and earthworks, it provided a strong point on the river line between Clifford and Chepstow and guarded two important river crossings.

The Wye was not only a valuable commercial trade route, it also provided easy access for raiding parties coming from the sea and looking for plunder. One such, a mixture of Danes, English and Welsh under Grufydd ap Llywelyn, did much damage to Archenfield in 1056. It is probable that the north wall of Dixton church, always an easy target from the river, was rebuilt after that raid. But as Domesday reports, 'as a result of the destruction the land was laid waste, therefore what it was like at that time is not known'. However, the herring bone masonry and the timber posts resting on it still remain to witness the rebuilding.

To the survivors of such raids there can have been little to choose between the advancing Normans and past oppressors, and the Earl of Hereford profited from the situation. He and his successors continued the pre-Conquest practice of allowing the men of Archenfield to retain their Welsh customs in return for military service. Although compelled to act as vanguard in the advance and rearguard in retreat, the bargain was not one-sided. Long after Welshmen further west had surrendered to Norman custom the men of Archenfield were enjoying their old and honoured tribal way of life. In the late fifteenth century the inhabitants still regarded it as an area where the King's writ could not be served.

Monmouth's strongest ties were with Archenfield and, as Norman policy there directly affected the town, some consideration must be given to the Earl of Hereford's dealings with it. The distinctive character of Archenfield was recognised by the compilers of the Domesday Survey when they divided the local landholders into separate categories; those of Herefordshire, Archenfield and Wales. Archenfield derived its name from the old Welsh commote of Erging, one of the cradles of Celtic Christianity.

The Domesday Survey devotes a section to the customs of Archenfield and, as they were those prevailing around Monmouth before the Conquest, their details are important.

In Archenfield the king has 3 churches. The priests of these churches bear the King's dispatches into Wales and each of them sings two masses each and every week for the king. If any one of them dies, the king has 20s from him by custom.

If any Welshman steals a man, a woman, a horse, an ox or a cow, when he is convicted of it, he first restores what he stole and gives 20s in forfeiture; but for stealing a sheep or a bundle of sheaves he pays a fine of 2s.

If anyone kills one of the King's men or commits house-breaking, he gives the king 20s as a payment for the man and 100s in forfeiture. If anyone has killed a thane's man, he gives 10s to the dead man's lord.

But if a Welshman has killed a Welshman, the relatives of the slain man gather and despoil the killer and his relatives and burn their houses until the body of the dead man is buried the next day about midday. The king has a third part of this plunder, but they have all the rest free.

Otherwise, a man who has burnt a house and is accused of it, proves his innocence through 40 men; but if he has been unable to, he will pay a fine of 20s to the king.

If anyone has concealed a sester of honey from the customary due and this is proved, he pays five sesters for one sester, if he holds as much land as ought to produce them.

If the Sheriff summons them to a meeting of the Shire, six or seven of the nobler ones of them go with him. A man who is called and does not go, gives 2s or one ox to the king; a man who stays away from the Hundred [meeting] pays as much.

Anyone who does not go when ordered by the Sheriff to go with him into Wales, is fined the same. But if the Sheriff does not go, none of them goes.

When the army advances on the enemy, these men by custom form the vanguard and on their return the rearguard.

These were the customs of the Welshmen in Archenfield T.R.E. (before 1066).

A further entry in Domesday Book makes clear that, apart from the honey rent, tenants in Archenfield paid only 20s instead of the sheep they used to

Dixton Church

The herring-bone masonry on the north wall of Dixton Church. Late eleventh century.

give, and 10s for smokesilver (the right to gather firewood). Otherwise they paid 'no geld nor any other customary due except that they will go forth in the king's army if commanded. If a free man dies there the king has his horse with armour. From the villain when he dies the king has one ox'.[1]

The honey rent was a survival of the Welsh *gwestva* or food rent. Honey was important, not only for sweetening and as an ingredient of mead, but because the candles for the Mass were made from beeswax. In the Gwentian Code the section on bees begins: 'The origin of bees is from Paradise, and on account of the sin of man they came thence, and they were blessed by God, and therefore the Mass cannot be without the wax'. In Archenfield ninety-six men with seventy-three ploughs paid 41 sesters of honey; in Monmouth, Welshmen holding twenty-four ploughs paid 33 sesters, and in Gwent the Welshmen paid 47 sesters. Honey survived in field names and there was still in this century a field at Hadnock called the Lower Honey Shares.

The custom which allowed a Welshman to plunder the kindred of the slayer of one of his family was, in effect, the right to wage private war, something which was appropriated on a large scale by the Marcher lords. And it was to Wales and the Welsh that many of these lords looked for their fighting men. The system was not peculiar to Archenfield but obtained in other commotes. Gradually the vendetta was replaced by the payment of compensation, the lord being entitled to one third.

The obligation to provide military service applied also to the Scottish border where, in Cumberland in 1212, tenants had to provide the vanguard when moving north and the rearguard on return.[2] The system in Herefordshire continued into the thirteenth century when Archenfield was held in sergeanty from the king by a community of Welshmen who were obliged by custom to furnish once a year, when the king required, fifty men for fifteen days against the Welsh at their own expense. Against England their service was limited to one day and night. They also paid 19 marks to the king each year, but owed no other services at all.

Archenfield today is a land of scattered farmsteads, dispersed settlements, isolated churches and Celtic place-names.[3] It was the centre of the cult of

Dyfrig (Dubricius) and as such a significant part of the Welsh church, but soon after its submission to the Normans it was incorporated into the diocese of Hereford. There it remained until 1844 when Monmouth and Dixton were detached from it and returned to Llandaff. This arrangement lasted less than a hundred years, and when in 1921 the Welsh diocese of Monmouth was formed, the parishes of Monmouth and Overmonnow became part of it, but the parishioners of Dixton and Wyesham voted themselves back to Hereford. This means that although the whole town lies in the county of Monmouth, about one third of the borough is in the Church of England. The fluctuations of the boundaries are an accurate reflection of the town's equivocal history.

William FitzOsbern died in Flanders in 1071 and was succeeded by his son Roger, 'a youth of hateful perfidy' who held the earldom until 1075 when he became involved in rebellion and was disgraced. No new earl was appointed and the Norman advance into South Wales came to a temporary halt. The

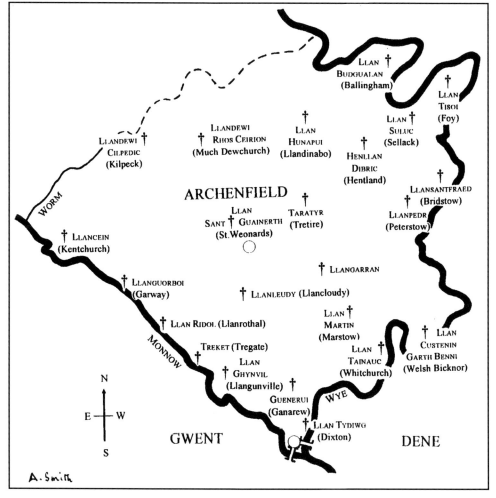

The churches of Archenfield. (A. Smith)

custodians of Monmouth Castle were involved in Roger's rebellion and, on their removal, the lordship was granted briefly to Ranulf de Colville.[4] Then, after some delay, permanent appointments were made and to Monmouth came a Breton called Gwethenoc, a man whose piety was to influence the town for the next two hundred years.[5] He was the son of Caradoc of Laboussac, an estate near Dol, and was born at a time when the noble families in that part of Brittany were engaged in a far-reaching monastic revival. He married a daughter of the Archbishop of Dol, had a brother and son who became monks, and when his work in Monmouth was ended he took the Benedictine vows. He was lord of Monmouth from c1075 until c1082, and the first of a Breton family which was to hold the lordship until 1256. Here the family could prosper; the Wye providing the town's commercial lifeblood, the castle helping to guard the frontier for the king, and the priory linking Monmouth with the outside world through its connection with France and the many local churches it would acquire.

2 The Priory

On Gwethenoc's arrival he lost little time in beginning what was to be his life's work, the founding of a Benedictine priory. He turned for help to a former neighbour, William of Dol, who had become Abbot of St. Florent at Saumur in 1070. From this great abbey on the Loire, 'The Glory of Anjou', William sent a prior and monks to inaugurate and serve the new priory, and in return, Monmouth Priory and its endowments were granted to St. Florent. This arrangement persisted until the fourteenth century, the priors of Monmouth coming usually from Saumur, and a proportion of Monmouth's income going annually to France. It was the second alien priory to be founded on the Lower Wye, being preceded only by FitzOsbern's foundation at Chepstow.

St. Florent, the founder of the parent abbey, was a disciple of St. Benedict and left Cassino in the sixth century to evangelise the Mauges region of France. His body was buried in a primitive church on Mons Glonna which in the seventh century became a monastery. From there the abbot sent monks to establish another house at Saumur, St. Hilary of the Caves. In the ninth century both Mons Glonna and St. Hilary were destroyed and the monks fled to Tournus. In c950 they returned to Saumur where the Count of Tours built them a monastery in his castle which became St. Florent du Chateau. It quickly became famous for its weaving and tapestry work. In turn it was destroyed but a new abbey was built in 1040, St. Florent de Saumur. Weaving and tapestry work continued and a great library was formed.

In Monmouth the priory church was not dedicated until 1101/2, so for over twenty years temporary accommodation was used. Initially the monks worshipped in the old Celtic church of St. Cadoc[6], beneath the slopes of the castle. (Appendix A) Subsequently they removed to the castle chapel after its dedication by Bishop Herwald of Llandaff in the presence of a Welsh prince, Caradoc ap Gruffydd.[7] If the book of Llandaff is to be believed about this dedication, it is early evidence of the cultural and religious bonds which united Welshmen and Bretons in this lordship. This Breton-Welsh harmony in Monmouth was matched and reinforced by the Norman-Welsh collaboration in Archenfield. Together they can only have intensified, to more patriotic Welshmen further west, the odour of treachery with which the area was becoming tainted. Traces of such distrust linger on.

After little more than seven years in Monmouth, Gwethenoc surrendered the lordship to the King, forsook the world, and retired to the abbey at Saumur which he had so richly endowed. It is doubtful whether he possessed the full powers of a Marcher lord as he had to seek personal confirmation of his grants of land from the King at Salisbury.[8] This rather unusual procedure for one whose rights over the disposal of his conquered lands should have been absolute, may have been due to the nature of his appointment and to the fact that the grants were going to Anjou, a state with which Normandy was then at odds.

Confirmation was granted by the King, Gwethenoc retired to Saumur and, as both his brother and his son were monks, he was succeeded by his nephew, William FitzBaderon, a powerful landowner whose interests were more secular than those of his uncle. It is possibly for this reason that Gwethenoc had to wait nineteen years in the cloisters of St. Florent before his priory church was completed and he could return to Monmouth for its dedication.

The Domesday Survey was not only concerned with the pre-conquest customs of Archenfield. More important to the king was the extent of the lordships at the time the survey occurred. William FitzBaderon held the lordship of Monmouth at the time and the entry is under Herefordshire:

In Monmouth Castle the king has four ploughs in lordship, William FitzBaderon has charge of them.
Value of what the king has in this castle, 100s. William has 8 ploughs in lordship; more possibly. There are Welshmen there who have 24 ploughs; they pay 33 sesters of honey and 2s.
15 slaves male and female; 3 mills at 20s.
William's men-at-arms have 7 ploughs. The value of what William holds is £30. St Florent de Saumur hold the church of the castle and all the tithe, with 2 carucates of land.
King Gruffydd and Bleddyn laid waste this land before 1066; therefore what it was like at that time is not known.

The land held by the king, the lord, the knights and the monks lay along the valley floor and was known as the Englishry. The land held by the Welsh consisted of the poorer uplands and became known as the Welshry or Patria. Such divisions survive in place-names like Welsh and English Newton and Welsh and English Bicknor. The plough or carucate, the area that one plough team could keep cultivated throughout the year, varied from place to place with the lie of the land and the nature of the soil. But, taking it to represent about 120 acres, it is possible to hazard a rough estimate of the size of the lordship at the time of Domesday.

Tenant	Ploughs	English Acreage	Welsh Acreage
The King	4	480	
The lord	8	960	
Knights	7	840	
Monks	2	240	
Welsh	24		2880
	45	2520	2880

Such figures are speculative and illustrate only the proportion of land held by English and Welsh. They give little indication of the comparative value of the holding, though the lord's, which was only twice the size of the king's, was six times as valuable. The statement that in the lord's demesne 'there could be more' may refer to the devastation caused earlier, but this is the only feature detracting from what appears to be a compact and flourishing agricultural community.

Moreover, there were in Monmouth itself, the triple foundations of the future town. There was the castle being built to provide defence and an administrative centre.[9] There was an embryo priory ensuring a constant stream of prayer for the souls of the inhabitants, and there was a market where the townspeople could buy the necessities of life. At first the market was held on the Great Causey (Monnow Street) but later it withdrew into the outer bailey of the castle.

3 The Borough

 While the castle and priory promised security in this world and the next, the market was the magnet designed to attract settlers to a dangerous outpost with an inhospitable climate. The lord controlled it and granted to suitable applicants rights to a burgage. This was an allotment near the market on which the burgess could build a tenement. As space near the market was limited in Monmouth by flooding and the early defences, the burgages were restricted in the amount of space they could occupy on the street. So the gable end faced the street and could be as little as 20 feet wide; access to the rear was by passages between the burgages. By the seventeenth century many burgages had become amalgamated or fragmented.[10]

Originally burgesses had a monopoly of trade, except on market days when they were excused the tolls paid by others. In return they had to pay an annual rent of 12 pence to the lord, unless they had been appointed by the prior. Soon after its establishment the priory had acquired the right to create burgesses, 'free from all toll and from all dues, save offences deserving corporal penalty'.[11](Appendix B) It was a privilege viewed with disfavour by the civic authorities, but in the eleventh century was an additional attraction for reluctant immigrants. By 1505, even the Knights of the Hospital of St. John at Dinmore and Garway owned a dozen burgages in Monmouth.[12]

The burgess system with its own official, the reeve, eventually became the borough with its mayor and bailiffs. But in the eleventh century it was part of a policy encouraged by William FitzOsbern when he introduced into this new settlement (as he did in Hereford) the Laws of Breteuil, a small town he owned in France. These laws, not at first available to Welshmen, offered inducements to merchants such as extra-mural land and immunity from interference. They were, however, obliged to give military service, being in effect a local militia. They were responsible for the defence of Monmouth and in 1402 had to pay £50 for the repair of the walls.[13]

The military aspect of the burgess system was responsible for the reluctance to grant the right to Welshmen. No Welshmen, according to one of Edward I's ordinances, could reside within a walled borough, and Monmouth's early charters stressed that burgesses could not be tried by Welshmen. Archaeological evidence confirms that all residents were at this time using pottery, a practice the Welsh found unnecessary. As a result Glyn Dwr saw burgesses as important targets because of their Englishness but, in spite of ordinances and attempts at discrimination, a fair proportion of Monmouth burgesses by 1400 had Welsh names.

The three elements - castle, priory and market - were eventually to make way for the manor, parish and borough, but the common heritage of religion, culture and language which united Breton and Celt was to bear fruit in the twelfth century.

William FitzBaderon built on the foundations laid by FitzOsbern and

Gwethenoc. At the castle the temporary wooden tower was protected above the Monnow by an escarpment of loose earth. This was always considered the danger area and, when the stone castle came to be built, the walls facing Wales were much thicker than those on the English side. In the town area the castle would have been guarded by a ditch, but there is little archaeological evidence for one, while the ditch along Nailers' Lane is flat bottomed and only a metre deep.

Whether FitzOsbern began the rebuilding of the castle in stone is hard to determine. If he did, only the lower ranges of the tower can be dated so far back. The tower, which is similar to, though better finished than that at Chepstow, may well have taken several years to build, and even if he began it, it is unlikely that FitzOsbern could have seen it completed.

Monmouth Castle, showing the thickness of the walls facing Wales.

Thus, when FitzBaderon succeeded in c1082, he probably inherited from Gwethenoc a tower used as a hall, a castle chapel, an uncompleted priory, a market for burgesses and a small town enclosed by ramparts, timber defences and water. He controlled a compact lordship, had extensive possessions in Herefordshire and Gloucestershire and was a man of sufficient eminence to attract to the dedication of his priory church in 1101 most of the important magnates from the surrounding countryside.[14]

The dedication of the priory church seems to have taken place at the same time that a grant of land on the Monnow belonging to William the Wise was officially recognised in 1101. The ceremony was conducted, appropriately, by Hervé, a Breton Bishop of Bangor who had been driven from his see by secular violence. Both the local bishops were debarred; Herwald of Llandaff because of his age and the fact that Monmouth was then firmly held as part of the diocese of Hereford, and Reynelm of that diocese because he was involved, on the wrong side, in a quarrel between the king and Anselm over ecclesiastical discipline.

Among the nobles present was Bernard, the King's Chaplain who, although a layman, had been made custodian of Hereford in Reynelm's absence. He was to become a great Bishop of St. David's, but at the time of the dedication he was a courtier and royal favourite. The Archdeacon of Hereford and other cathedral dignitaries accompanying him were showing the diocesan flag in what had recently been disputed territory. Harold of Ewyas, lord of one of the earliest Norman estates in England, was there, and so was the founder of Abergavenny priory, Hamelin de Balaon. One of the latter's sisters was married to Walter FitzRoger, Sheriff of Gloucester and Constable of England, who was also present. With him came the Conqueror's old chaplain, Serlo, Abbot of Gloucester, the builder of the great nave of what was to become the cathedral. He was accompanied by Walter de Lacy, who became Abbot of Gloucester in 1130.

From Monmouth came Hugo the steward and several members of the lord's family; his wife Hadwise, with their son Evennus Trouet and their daughters, Advenia and Iveta. The three woman made the large crosses which can be seen at the bottom of the document describing the ceremony. The lord's brother Payn was also there. From Saumur came the abbot, William of Dol who, since sending the first monks to Monmouth, had become one of the most eminent and revered figures in the Loire valley. Finally came Gwethenoc, the founder of the church, probably visiting Monmouth for the last time.

All of them witnessed the grant to the church of the land of William the Wise. Such grants were usually symbolised by the placing of some object on the altar, generally a knife but sometimes a book or ring.[15] Bernard was responsible for this part of the ceremony which was normally well rehearsed and involved the breaking of the knife. Unfortunately for Bernard he had difficulty in doing this and the charter records that 'he broke [it] with his foot because he could not break it with his hands'.

The knife symbolised the cutting away of the land from its previous owner; the breaking of it that it could never be severed from the new owner. It is similar to the breaking of a wine glass at a Jewish wedding as a sign that the union shall last as long as the glass remains broken. There are further parallels with the handing over of a rod by customary tenants when disposing of their land in Monmouth.

Little remains of the original church. The respond in the present building is part of the twelfth century nave and the chevron string course on the tower is later than 1115. The rubble masonry at the base of the tower may well go back to 1100. The building was in decay before the Dissolution. Both

.Willm.

[Medieval Latin charter text in manuscript hand]

The charter referring to the dedication of the Priory church c1101.

William son of Baderon gave also, on the banks of the Monnow, the land of William called the Wise (Sapiens) to St. Florent at the dedication of St. Mary's church. The gift is witnessed by Hervey, bishop of Bangor, by whom the church was dedicated; also by Bernard, the king's chaplain, who then, by command of King Henry, had the custody of the see of Hereford; lastly by Heinfrid the archdeacon, Walter the canon, Gunfrei, Ketelbern priest and canon, Harald of Ewias, Hamelin de Balaon, Walter the Sheriff, Eutropius, Harscotus Musard: (and) of William's tenants, Payn his brother, Robert son of Bernardi, Evennus Trouet, Hugh dapifer, and many others.

This charter, with all the gifts previously mentioned, was confirmed by William son of Baderon, and Hadwise his wife, and their daughters Iveta and Advenia, in the sight of William abbot of St. Florent and Serlo abbot of Gloucester and in sight of their monks, namely: (of St. Florent) Wihenoc the monk, Unbald, Donatus, Rannulfus, Gislebertus, Maino, Samuel; of the monks of abbot Serlo, Walter de Laci, Restoldus and others; Teodericus monk of Cormeilles, Odo the monk.

They made this gift and grant also in the sight of all those both clerk and lay, who were present at the dedication. This grant was made by (the symbol of) a knife, which Bernard the king's chaplain, broke beneath his foot, because he could not break it with his hands; by which knife, placed upon the altar, William son of Baderon, with his wife and daughters, made this gift sure, as a testimony for the future.

+   +   +

Has cruces fecerunt Domina Hadewis et filiae ejus, Iveta
videlicet et Advenia.

(Original in archives of Maine et Loire, J.H. Round, op. cit., p.408)

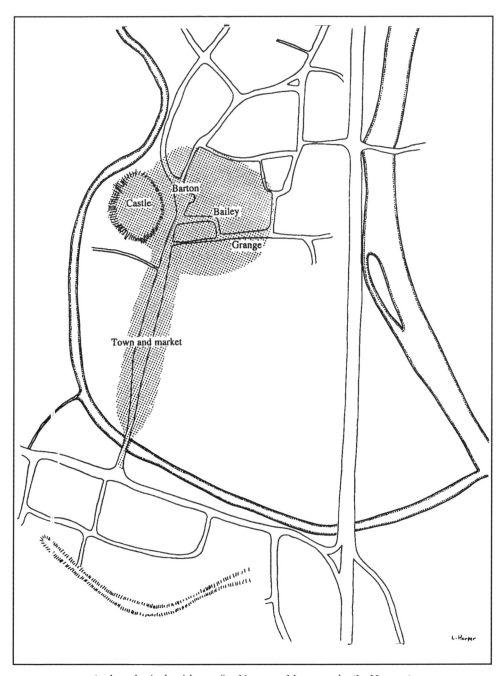

Archaeological evidence for Norman Monmouth. (L. Harper)

John Speed in 1610 and Thomas Dyneley in 1684 show only the ruined arcade still standing. But in the twelfth century it was new and important and as its importance increased so did its endowments. These gifts, which included land, mills, forges, weirs, rents, burgages and tithes, impoverished the churches from which they came.

Around Monmouth it was the Celtic church which was most affected. It found a champion in Urban, Bishop of Llandaff who, in 1119, persuaded Pope Calixtus II to warn the Marcher lords, including FitzBaderon, 'The complaint of your mother the church of Llandaff has come to us, because it is plundered of its property by you, and reduced to almost nothing...Therefore we command that you restore without delay the lands, tithes...and other property which you have wickedly taken away...Otherwise we will confirm against you, as...persons guilty of sacrilege, the sentence which our venerable brother Urban, your bishop, has with canonical justice promulgated'.[16]

This was less than Urban had hoped for, and although it was repeated in 1128, it was singularly ineffective. Churches, land and tithes continued to be granted to Monmouth Priory and through it to the parent abbey in France. The ruthlessness with which the appropriation of these churches was pursued is well illustrated by William II's grant of Andover to St. Florent at Saumur. The King directed that 'all the churches built under the mother church of Andover should be utterly destroyed or should be held by the monks of St. Florent'.[17] That charter was witnessed by Alan, Count of Brittany[18] and by Gwethenoc who was then a monk at Saumur. These two had been present in the King's Chamber at Salisbury in the early days when the Conqueror had confirmed Gwethenoc's grants of land and tithes to the priory. They and their successors were unlikely to be deterred by pronouncements from Rome.

William FitzBaderon was succeeded by his eldest son Baderon in c1125. His first act was to receive the declaration of homage and fealty from his men. This normally took place at the castle gate where his authority was acknowledged by the customary renders of dues and gifts. He confirmed the possessions of the priory which had been granted by his predecessors, and added the tithes of hay and hunting, along with some land at Hadnock and the weir at Brockweir.[19]

Further endowments came from his sister Margaret who had married as her second husband Hugh FitzRichard of Hatton in Worcestershire. She persuaded her husband to endow the priory with lands and churches in that diocese because one of three sons by a previous marriage, Robert, had become Prior of Monmouth. There were few members of this large Breton family who did not contribute towards the welfare of Gwethenoc's foundation.

Between 1138 and 1148 Baderon married Rohesia, the daughter of the lord of Chepstow. The espousal took place at Chepstow on All Saints Day and was marked by a gift to Monmouth Priory, a gift which was confirmed ten days later in Monmouth by placing a knife on the altar there.[20] This time no attempt was made to break it. Although the bride's mother was present, her father, Gilbert Strongbow, was not, and she was given away by an uncle. Amongst the guests and witnesses were Odo, prior of Chepstow, and Geoffrey, Prior of Monmouth. Geoffrey the Prior is not to be confused with Geoffrey the Chronicler who was alive at that time. It is perhaps significant that in one of the charters Geoffrey the prior is referred to as Goffredus Parvus.

St. Mary's Church in 1684 by Thomas Dineley.

Nevertheless, by about 1139, Geoffrey of Monmouth had produced his *Historia Regum Britanniae*, 'History of the Kings of Britain', and it was on its way to becoming one of the most widely distributed books of the Middle Ages. He described himself in his literary works as Galfridus Monemutensis.

On the other hand when his name appears as a witness to a charter, it is always Galfridus Artur. Although Artur at that time was a common Breton name, he may have used it as a nickname. William of Newburgh implies this when he states that 'This man is called Geoffrey, having the by-name, Arthur, because by the added veneer of the Latin language he cloaked in the respectable name of history the fables about Arthur taken from ancient fictions of the British and augmented from his own resources'.

It seems probable that he was born in Monmouth of Breton parents and then moved to Oxford where he wrote his book. He dedicated it to Henry I's natural son, Robert, Earl of Gloucester, and in calling him 'a secondary Henry' underlined his admiration for a king who had died before the book was finished.

What then was it all about? And why did it prove so popular? Briefly, Geoffrey told of the arrival of Brutus from Troy, his defeat of the local giants, and his founding of New Troy here in Britain. When he died the kingdom, apart from Cornwall, was divided between his three sons: Locrine obtaining England, Albanect Scotland and Camber Wales. Amongst their many successors were Ebrancus who founded York, Bladud who founded Bath, and Lear, the father of Regan, Goneril and Cordelia.

Throughout the story, Cornwall plays an important part as the home of the true Britons. Their heroes, Dunwallo Molmutius, Brennus, Asclepiodotus, fought continuously to defend the country from Romans and Saxons. It was not until Arthur was crowned by Dubricius at Caerleon that, in alliance with the Bretons, he conquered the known world before being wounded and carried to Avalon. Although this was the end of Arthur, it was not the end of the struggle, as fresh waves of invading Saxons drove the Britons back to their strongholds in Cornwall and Wales. The Britons then became the Welsh and finally their leader Cadwaladr sought help and refuge in Brittany. There he was assured by an angel that one day the Britons would regain their inheritance and that the prophecies of Merlin would be fulfilled, 'when the appointed time should come'.[21]

It was a book which satisfied the mediaeval love of pedigrees, provided Britain with a splendidly imaginative past and gave the true Britons the promise of an eventual return to power. Three hundred and fifty years after it was written, Henry Tudor landed in Wales from Brittany and, marching under the Red Dragon of Cadwaladr, won back for the true line the Crown of England on Bosworth Field. Using Geoffrey to bolster his claim to the throne, he called his first-born Arthur.

The Tudors were not alone in using the British History, as it was soon called. Within fifteen years of its appearance it had spread through Europe and no man was considered educated who had not read it. Sceptics such as William of Newburgh were dismissed, and the History received fresh confirmation with the discovery of Arthur's body at Glastonbury. There the monks, with a shrine on their hands which could rival Becket's, elaborated the legend. Arthur became a descendant of Joseph of Arimathaea who had married the daughter of the spearman at the Crucifixion and who in turn was a natural son of Julius Caesar. Excalibur was unearthed and presented by Richard I to Tancred of Sicily, and the British History, revered by Church and State, became something which only the occasional noble critic, like Humphrey of Gloucester, dared to question.

Diplomatically it was invaluable. Glyn Dwr, when seeking an alliance with Robert III of Scotland, used their common descent from Brutus as an inducement; and in the fifteenth century it provided much of the ammunition in the prolonged dispute over the antiquity of Oxford and Cambridge. The Renaissance might have laughed it out of court, but a foreigner, Polydore Vergil, chose this time to attack it and the normally contentious British antiquaries immediately united in its defence. Leland, Lambarde, Holinshed, Caius, Humphry Lhuyd and Richard White committed themselves to what Geoffrey had written, while others like John Bayle improved on the original by tracing the British kings back to Noah by way of Shem, Ham, Japhet, Amphitrite, Isis, Osiris and the King of the Isles of the Sea.[22]

Not until Camden published his *Britannia* in 1586 did an antiquary of note take up Polydore Vergil's criticism and admit there was justification for it. But Camden's doubts did not prevent Queen Elizabeth incorporating Brutus, Belinus, Arviragus and Arthur in one of her coats of arms, nor Sir Roger Williams of Penrhos in Monmouthshire in 1596 tracing his family back to Brutus by way of Locrine, Camber and Albanect.[23] Nor did it prevent John Milton, whose *History of Britain* was published in 1670, reproducing a great deal of Geoffrey quite uncritically.

But by the time Archdeacon Coxe was touring at the end of the eighteenth century, most antiquaries had become dubious, though many of their theories were as fanciful as the British History itself. Thus Coxe: 'The controversy is finally decided and the best Welsh critics allow that Geoffrey's work was a vitiated translation of the British Kings written by Tyssilo…who flourished in the seventh century…We may therefore conclude that Geoffrey ought to be no more cited as historical authority than Amadis de Gaul or the Seven Champions of Christendom'.[24] In fact, Tyssilo's manuscript was merely a Welsh translation of the British History, and Coxe's theories were typical of many then prevalent, including those of Charles Heath, the Monmouth antiquary who thought Geoffrey was also Giraldus.[25]

Geoffrey became archdeacon of Llandaff in 1140 and died in 1155, consecrated but never instituted to the see of St. Asaph. His influence on mediaeval thought and literature was considerable. Drayton, Spenser, Shakespeare and Milton owed much to his stories. The years of Geoffrey's success coincided with the enrichment and extension of the priory which, by the end of the century was at its greatest. The fullest account of its possessions is in a bull of Urban III, dated 1186.[26] Supplementing it from other charters kept in France, a fairly complete list of churches belonging to it can be seen:

In Hereford diocese: St. Nicholas, Staunton; St. Roald, (Llanrothal) with its chapels of St. Michael (Llangunville) and St. Thomas, Treget; St. Giles, Goodrich with its chapel of Houson (Huntsham); St. John, Hope Mansell; St. Margaret, Tibberton; St. Peter, Tadyngton (Tarrington); St. George, Clun 'with all the churches of all the vills belonging to the castle'; St. Custenin, Biconovria (Welsh Bicknor); Llangarren; Album Monasterium (Whitchurch); St. Andrew, Awre, with the land called Hayward; Lindeneia Baderonis (St. Briavels); the chapel of Hiweldestun (Hewelsfield) with its chapel of Ashperton.
In Llandaff diocese: St. Cadoc, Llangattock with its chapel of St. Liwit, (Llanllwydd); St. Thomas, Newcastle and St. Mohan of Llanmohan (St. Maughans); St. Kinephaut, Rockfield; St. John of Troia (Troy); St. Brigid, Skenfrith; St. Guingalous, Wonastow; the chapel of St. Thomas, Panrox (Penrhos).
In other dioceses: St. Michael, Claverdon, with all its chapels; Hatton,

with the castle chapel of St. John; St. Radegund, Grayingham (Lincs); Siddington; Weston-Under-Edge; Morton (Birtsmorton); Hinton (Dorset); St. Nicholas, Halduvestre, (Austrey, Warwicks).

To these must be added the Monmouth churches which in 1186 were: 'The church of St. Mary of Monmouth with the chapels of St. Thomas and St. Duellus', and 'The church of St. Peter, Tadioc with the chapels of St. Thomas, Ganarew, St. Thomas, Wyesham, Garth and Colmanville'. There was also a chapel in the castle, so that although St. Cadoc had disappeared, there were still eight places of worship within an area of about 3 square miles.

St. Mary of Monmouth was the parish church while its chapel of St. Thomas at Overmonnow had been dedicated to Becket soon after his death. His cult was then flourishing and commemorated at Wyesham, Ganarew, Newcastle, Treget and Penrhos. St. Thomas, Overmonnow was on the wrong side of the river to remain long in the diocese of Hereford and was treated as belonging to Llandaff in the next century. The north door and the chancel arch of the original building remain. St. Duellus stood above the river Trothy and until 1956 part of it was still standing. It was then bulldozed into its nearby well and all that now survives are the names, St. Dials Farm and

The church of St. Thomas at Overmonnow (c. 1186) after its first restoration in 1829 by T. H. Wyatt. The Duke of Beaufort's timber wagons, drawn by mixed teams of oxen and horses, did great damage going round corners. In self-defence many people living on corners deliberately rounded them, as at the top of St. Mary Street.

Holywell Wood. One of the few examples of the work of the Herefordshire School of Romanesque Sculptors, dating from c1150, was found in a brick wall in Monnow Street. It may have come from the new church of St. Mary. St. Peter, Tadioc is Llantyddwg (Dixton) and shows its Celtic founder in

Romanesque carving by one of the Herefordshire School c1150 found in a wall in Monnow Street.

Carving on the font at Eardisley c1150 showing a similar scene, in this case the Harrowing of Hell.

transition from saint to place-name. This fleeting conjunction between the Norman favourite, Peter, and the obscure Welshman led in the next century to St. Peter Tydiucston and then, when the Ty- was dropped, through Diucston, Dukeston, Duxton to Dixton.

Of Dixton's four chapels, Ganarew had become a separate parish by 1340.[27] Garth, traditionally a hermitage, lay on the site of the farm of that name across the river. Colmanvill (Villa Colman) has left few traces but the Colman rocks on the Wye below Penalt had a chapel dedicated to St. Denis nearby. St. Thomas, Wyesham is now a house called The Cell about two hundred yards from the nineteenth century church of St. James. It became known as King's Chapel and in the eighteenth century served as parsonage, poor house and, eventually, a private house. When the last transformation took place the stone altar slab was still at the east end, there was a large three-light window under the plaster, and a small single-light window which can still be seen.

The extensive material possessions of the priory were matched by considerable spiritual and literary activity. Some time after 1175 a liturgical kalendar, with an accompanying collection of the lives of certain Welsh and Breton saints, was compiled, probably in Monmouth.[28] It omits almost all the accepted festivals of the Roman kalendar and includes those of some thirty Celtic saints. In this it resembles the type of kalendar which preceded the reforms of Charlemagne, and has more in common with the ninth century than the twelfth. This unique document, celebrating saints who were as well known locally as they were in Brittany, seems to have been one of the more significant results of the policy of enlightened colonialism practised by the Breton invaders of Monmouth.

Although the most influential element in the town during the twelfth century was the priory, both castle and market were increasing in importance. Moreover the marriage of Baderon with Rohesia of Chepstow allayed anxiety about this powerful neighbour whose boundary ran within a mile of Monmouth Castle. By 1166 Baderon answered to the king for fifteen knight's fees and thereafter this was the usual demand made upon the lordship.[29]

The castle buildings, as far as one can tell, consisted of the original Great Hall or Tower begun by FitzOsbern, a gatehouse with nearby chapel built by Gwethenoc and a curtain wall. The surviving string course of the hall and the single-light windows are part of the original building. It was of two storeys with an entrance on the second, probably on the south wall. This storey contained the principal rooms with slightly larger windows than those of the undercroft. The west wall overlooked the Monnow, and stood above a scarped embankment. There was a small extension, probably to protect the entrance, but it was demolished when the second hall was added in the thirteenth century. The outer defences of the town at this time were probably still of earth and timber. The ditches seem to have been abandoned on the street frontage near Lloyds Bank in the middle of the twelfth century. The same ditch at the top of Chippenhamgate Street may have remained open longer.

Inside the castle was a notable library, 'rich in books both Latin and

Romance', belonging to Lord Gilbert who had succeeded his father, Baderon c1176. The library is referred to by a metrical poet, Hue de Roteland, whose patron, Gilbert had lent him a book which he had translated from Latin into Romance.[30] It is a long poem called *Prothesilaus* and is dedicated to Gilbert who is thanked for his generosity. He was also a benefactor of Flaxley Abbey, leaving to the monks there money to repair their books.[31] He may well have been instrumental in encouraging the monks in Monmouth to compile their liturgical kalendar.

Before becoming Lord of Monmouth, Gilbert witnessed one of his father's charters which is of interest because it concerns the twelfth century iron trade

The Great Tower of the Castle c1120-50.

and provides an early reference to the sale of iron for profit. It is dated between 1166 and 1176 and begins with a greeting to all friends and neighbours, 'French, English and Welsh'.[32] It grants to Monmouth Priory three forges, valued at 20s each, on the banks of the Wye. There is to be freedom of the wharf for all those buying and selling iron, and freedom of toll unless iron is being sold at a profit. No forestage was to be paid on the charcoal used in the forges and conditions were laid down to ensure that they did not fall into decay or prove detrimental to the lord. (Appendix D)

Excavations between the Wye and the town have provided evidence of the extent of these iron workings and the length of time they were in use. By Baderon's accession there were others as well as the three given to the monks. One of them was granted to William de Mareis in exchange for a white horse and a silver ring. At the other side of the town in Overmonnow recent excavations by the Monmouth Archaeological Society have uncovered a group of late thirteenth century iron workers' premises. They consist of mainly wooden buildings erected on sleeper beams and aligned along the road side. They were open-sided and contained at least five iron-working hearths, set on pits filled with clay. As on the Wye, signs of Roman occupation were also evident.[33]

The ore came from the Doward and the Forest of Dean but, as the method used by both Romans and Bretons was wasteful, large drifts of discarded 'cinders' were formed. They can be seen on the river banks in Speed's map of Monmouth in 1610. They were used as foundations for walls and buildings until, in the eighteenth century, it was found that the cinders contained enough iron to make it worth while selling them to the more efficient furnaces in the Lower Wye Valley. Once this was known, the citizens indulged in an orgy of digging, the remains of the town walls, islands in the rivers and many early buildings disappearing in the process. Cinderhill Street, now perfectly flat, commemorates the industry in Overmonnow as surely as Ironmongers Lane (Granville Street) confirms the site of the forges on the Wye.

Apart from his interest in literature, little is known about the lord Gilbert. He married Berta, a lady who, according to Giraldus, had the curious distinction of being a monk of Abbey Dore. Giraldus, who was no friend of the Cistercians, noted that she was 'solemnly hooded and made into a monk, not without giving scandal; [the monks] making a firm promise of the gate of heaven opening for her soul'.[34] This singular honour may have been due to the fact that Dore's first colony at Grace Dieu was built by Berta's son, John of Monmouth. He was under age when his father died in 1189/90 and was made the ward of his uncle, William de Braose, who paid a thousand marks for the privilege. John held the lordship for nearly fifty years and during that time the town grew to be an important pocket of loyalty in the increasingly unstable southern march.

He was still in ward when King John came to the throne, his uncle paying the scutage on his lands; but by 1201 he had married Cecily, the daughter of Walter de Waleran, and had paid the king 120 marks and 2 Norway hawks for her share of her father's lands.[35] When she died in 1222 he married Agnes, the daughter of Walter de Musgros, by whom he had three sons.

Almost alone amongst the Breton Lords of Monmouth, he played a part in national affairs outside the Marches. King John visited Monmouth on a hunting expedition in 1213.[36] When he lay dying three years later at Newark, the Lord of Monmouth, one of the executors of his will, was at his bedside.[37] John was also present in Gloucester Cathedral when the nine-year-old Henry was crowned with 'a sort of chaplet'; and he carried one of the four silver spears which supported the canopy over Queen Eleanor at her coronation. He was custodian of many forests, Constable of St. Briavels[38], provided the miners for the siege of Newark[39] and, on the rebellion of Richard the Marshal in 1233, he became one of the King's chief lieutenants in South Wales.

The rebellion of the great marshal was due in part to an influx of Poitevins into the Marches after the fall of the Justiciar, Hubert de Burgh. One of these interlopers was Baldwin de Guisnes, a soldier of fortune who had been allowed into England in 1227 and then given command of a mixed force of Flemings and Poitevins in Monmouth castle. The surrounding countryside from Chepstow to Grosmont was controlled by Richard, and it was his diversion, when returning from a foraging expedition near Skenfrith, which led to a brief and bitter battle with the Monmouth garrison on St. Catherine's Day in 1233. The encounter is well described by Roger of Wendover.[40]

Richard, whose main body had gone on towards Chepstow, on reaching Monmouth took a reconnaissance party of about a hundred men to the far side of the Castle Field. They were seen by Baldwin from the castle and he immediately took a party over the castle bridge in the hope of taking hostages. As he was outnumbered, Richard was urged to flee but, answering that he had never turned his back on an enemy, he rode into battle. The fight lasted for most of the day and was remarkable for the ease with which Richard outwitted his opponent. On one occasion he was attacked by Baldwin and twelve of his men, and his horse was killed under him, 'but the marshal, who was well practised in the French way of fighting, seized one of the knights...by his feet, dragged him to the ground, and then quickly mounting his adversary's horse, he renewed the battle'. This so infuriated Baldwin that he 'made a desperate attack on him, and seizing his helmet, tore it from his head with such violence that blood gushed forth from his mouth and nostrils; he then seized the marshal's horse by the bridle and endeavoured to drag it with its rider towards the castle, while others assisted by impelling the marshal from behind. The latter however, sweeping his sword behind him, struck two of his enemies to the earth stunned, but could not then release himself from their grasp'. A crossbowman came to the rescue by wounding Baldwin and, as he collapsed, Richard escaped.

By then the main body had returned and, on their arrival, the Poitevins fled over the castle bridge with their prisoners. In the stampede the bridge collapsed and many fell into the Monnow. Others were cut off or killed but Baldwin escaped, being carried back wounded to the castle. It was not the end of his mercenary career and he was back in England in 1267 at the head of another band.

The victors followed up their success by devastating the countryside 'so that the whole atmosphere in that part of the country was tainted by the number of dead foreigners who lay about in the roads and other places'. In the following year John of Monmouth, who had been notably absent when his castle was under attack, returned to conduct operations in person. He set out to ambush the enemy but was himself surprised near Trellech when Richard's forces 'rushed on them amidst the din of horns and trumpets and, taking them unawares, soon put them to flight'. John escaped with his life, but his lands and possessions were pillaged, 'thus making him a poor man and a beggar, instead of a rich man as he had been'.

The situation was saved by the treacherous murder of the marshal in Ireland, and John was meagrely rewarded for his inglorious campaign by the King's gift of a horse worth 30 marks.[41] Apart from the castle bridge which collapsed, other buildings which suffered were St. Thomas's church at Overmonnow which was set on fire and the newly-founded Cistercian Abbey of Grace Dieu which was destroyed. The King sent 13 great oaks from the Forest of Dean for the repair of the church[42] but Grace Dieu was a more serious loss.[43] It was completely demolished by the marshal's Welsh ally, Llywelyn ap Iorwerth, on the grounds that it had been built on land seized from the Welsh by John of Monmouth. John had founded it in 1226 some three miles west of Monmouth and staffed it with monks from Dore, which became the mother house. The king made grants of timber for its repair on three occasions but, in 1236, John rebuilt it on a nearby site and ordered the abbot to meet Llywelyn at Montgomery to arrange for compensation.

It was Llywelyn who, on the marshal's death, became John's most serious opponent. In 1236 John was ordered to 'provide for the sufficient defence of the March...and resist the said Llywelyn at an opportune season'.[44] In the next few years John's power increased rapidly. Chepstow, Usk, Caerleon, Cardigan and Carmarthen came temporarily under his control,[45] and in 1242 he was made Chief Bailiff of South Wales. He had captured Builth in the previous year and was ordered to provide 500 Welsh soldiers 'for the expected war with France'[46], followed by a further 2,000 for service in Gascony.[47] In Welsh affairs he was authorised to receive the assistance of the sheriffs of Worcester, Gloucester and Hereford.[48] The last named could still invoke the customs of Archenfield as laid down in Domesday Book.[49]

John was the most important of the Breton lords from a national rather than a local stand point. He died in 1248 and was buried in St Mary's Church. Thomas Dineley made a drawing of his tomb in 1684 after Parliamentary soldiers had defaced it, but before the restorers of 1737 had abolished it completely.[50]

John was succeeded by his eldest son, also called John of Monmouth. He held the lordship for little more than eight years and then surrendered it to the king in exchange for some land in Wiltshire and Dorset.[51] He died the

John of Monmouth's tomb in St. Mary's Church (after Thomas Dineley, 1684).

following year and 'whatever belongs to the king, of the castle, town and honour of Monmouth' was granted to the Lord Edward.[52] It was a century in which death played havoc with the Marcher families and in most cases it was the king who benefited.

The reasons for surrender of the lordship are obscure. It may have been ill-health since John died without male heirs a year later. More probably it was debt. Hereford money-lenders were powerful at that time and the matter arose again when the lordship passed from Edward to his brother Edmund. In 1270, just before he left for the Holy Land, the latter was pardoned a debt to the Exchequer of over £1,777, 'for divers debts wherein John of Monmouth who sometime held the Honour was bound at the Exchequer on the day of his death'.[53] The size of the debt may have been due to devastation of the lordship at the time of the rebellion of the earl marshal. But it was not uncommon for Henry III to involve his barons in debts which they had little hope of repaying as a means of infiltrating the royal presence into the March. If this was the explanation it was a sad quietus for a family which had been generous to the town and consistently loyal to the crown.

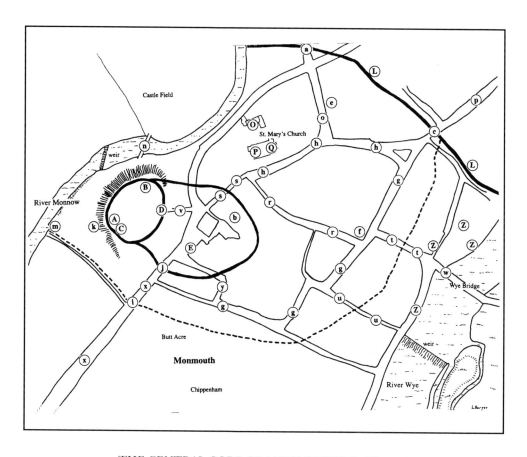

THE CENTRAL CORE OF MONMOUTH (L. Harper)

A	The Great Tower (1100-1150)	m	Castle Mill
B	The Round Tower (c1250)	n	Castle Bridge
C	The Great Hall (c1270)	o	Monk Street
D	Castle Gate & Chapel	p	Peter's Lane to Dixton
E	Market Place	r	St. Mary Street
O,P,Q	Priory and parish church	s	Butchers' Row
Z	Industrial area of wharves, etc.	t	Wyebridge Street
a	Monk's Gate	u	Weirhead Street
b	The Barton	v	Castle Bailey Street
c	Dixton or East Gate	w	Monmouth Bridge
e	Priory Infirmary	x	Monnow Street
f	The Grange	y	Inch Lane
g	Greindor (Glendower Street)		
h	Whitecross Street	Ⓛ ———	Line of wall according to Leland
I	Gate in Town Wall		
j	St. Stephen's or Burnt Gate		
k	St. Cadoc's Church?	- - - - - -	Possible line of town wall

REFERENCES Part One

(Abbreviations for some of the more frequently cited sources appear on page 8)

[1]   Domesday Book: Herefordshire. (Phillimore).
[2]   C. W. Hollister, *The Military Organisation of Norman England.*
[3]   For the Welsh place-names of Archenfield see B.G. Charles, *Angles and Britons*, U.W.P., 1965, pp.85-96.
[4]   LL, p.278.
[5]   See Reverend S. M. Harris in JHSCW, vol. III, no.8, p.14.
[6]   Dugdale, *Monasticon*, IV, p.595. When the Reverend William Cole visited Monmouth in 1743 he was shown outhouses 'anciently a church dedicated to St. Cadoc' (BM Add. MS 5811).
[7]   LL, p.278.
[8]   *Calendar of Documents in France,* p.407. (No. 1135).
[9]   See D. F. Renn, 'The Anglo-Norman Keep, 1066-1138' in *Journal of Brit. Arch. Assoc.*, vol. XXIII, 1960.
[10] This complicated the voting qualifications of the occupants.
[11] CDF, p.406. (No. 1133).
[12] Rental Book of the Preceptory of Dynmore and Garway, 1505. Hereford Record Office, A63/3/Box 104, p.27.
[13] DL, 42/15, fol.170.
[14] CDF, p.408. The dating of the dedication depends on two adjacent charters in the archives of Maine et Loire, (numbered 3 and 4), describing an event for which the same lords 'had then come to Monmouth'. Both charters are dated 1101/2.
[15] Tarrington was given to Monmouth by placing the Gospels on the altar; Awre by a gold ring.
[16] LL, p.93.
[17] CDF, p.415.
[18] Alan Dapifer (or Steward) of Dol, whose descendants became the Stuarts of Scotland.
      J. H. Round, *Studies in Peerage and Family History*, Constable, 1901.
[19] CDF, p.412.
[20] J. G. Wood, *The Lordship, Castle and Town of Chepstow*, which has a photograph of the charter (P.R.O. Cartae Antiquae 399). Rohesia outlived Baderon and on his death married Hugh de Lacy by whom she had four sons. She died c1180.
[21] The *Vita Merlini*, a long Latin poem appeared c1149. The Prophecies of Merlin was incorporated in later editions of the History.
[22] See *British Antiquity* by T. D. Kendrick (Methuen, 1950) for the best account of the influence of the British History.
[23] *Proceedings of the Monmouth and Caerleon Antiquarian Assoc.*, 1927-28, p.27.
[24] *Historical Tour through Monmouthshire*, 1801, p.243.
[25] *Account of the Ancient and Present State of Monmouth*, 1804.
[26] CDF, p.404. (No. 1129).
[27] In 1825 a large part of the original church 'fell down during divine service without any consequence but temporary alarm to the congregation'. (*Hereford Journal*, 31/8/1825).
[28] See Reverend S. M. Harris, *op. cit.*, and Kathleen Hughes in *Studies in the Early British Church*, 1958, pp.183-200. BM MS Cotton Vespasian, A xiv (Vitae Sanctorum Wallensium).
[29] Red Book, pp.280-1, Pipe Roll 14 Henry II, p.116. By 1229 the muster roll shows the lord of Monmouth providing only 3 knights (P.R.O. C72/2, m.21) but as the Earl of Hereford only provided 5, this may have been concerted evasion.
[30] *Prothesilaus*: MS Coton, Vespasian, A, vii fo. 37-104. It is transcribed for the most part in *Metrical Romances* by H. Webber, Edinburgh, 1910.
[31] A. W. Crawley-Boevey, *Cartulary and Historical Notes on the Cistercian Abbey of Flaxley*, 1887, p.133.

[32]   Dugdale, *Monasticon* IV, p.596.

[33]   S. Clarke, 'Recent Archaeological Work in Monmouth' in *Archaeology in Wales*, vol. 31, 1991.

[34]   *Speculum Ecclesiae.*

[35]   Thomas Wakeman, 'On the Priory of Monmouth'.

[36]   *Introduction to Patent Rolls*, p.54.

[37]   M. Powicke, *The Thirteenth Century*, Clarendon Press, p. 3.

[38]   Cal. Patent Rolls, 1216-1225, p.419.

[39]   P.R.O. C 72/2 m. 22.

[40]   *The Flowers of History*, II, p.574. Bohn, 1849.

[41]   Close Roll. Henry III. p. 371.

[42]   Close Roll. 18 Henry III.

[43]   For the history of its foundation see D. Williams, 'Grace Dieu Abbey' in *Monmouthshire Antiquary*, I (1964), part 4.

[44]   Cal. Patent Rolls. 1232-1247, p.235.

[45]   Ibid. pp.254, 276.

[46]   Ibid. pp.196.

[47]   Cal. Close Rolls. 1242-1247. p. 76.

[48]   Cal. Patent Rolls. 1232-1247. p. 289.

[49]   Cal. I.P.M. Henry III, No. 20, p.6.

[50]   *Account of the Official Progress of His Grace the first Duke of Beaufort through Wales in 1684*, p. 386.

[51]   Cal. I.P.M. Henry III, no. 311, p.101. Marriage of his widow, Isabel, was granted to Baldwin de Vile and his lands in Dorset and Wiltshire passed to his daughters, Lady Alberta de Boterell and Lady Joan Neville.

[52]   Close Roll. 40 Henry III.

[53]   Cal. Liberate Rolls, 1 March 1269, p.116 and Cal. Patent Rolls, 1266-1272, pp.418, 419.

THE BRETON LORDS OF MONMOUTH

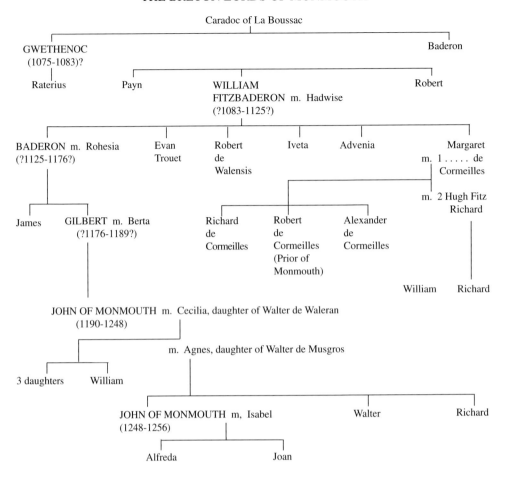

Caradoc of La Boussac

GWETHENOC (1075-1083)? — Baderon

Raterius — Payn — WILLIAM FITZBADERON m. Hadwise (?1083-1125?) — Robert

BADERON m. Rohesia (?1125-1176?) — Evan Trouet — Robert de Walensis — Iveta — Advenia — Margaret m. 1 ..... de Cormeilles / m. 2 Hugh Fitz Richard

James — GILBERT m. Berta (?1176-1189?) — Richard de Cormeilles — Robert de Cormeilles (Prior of Monmouth) — Alexander de Cormeilles — William — Richard

JOHN OF MONMOUTH m. Cecilia, daughter of Walter de Waleran (1190-1248)

m. Agnes, daughter of Walter de Musgros

3 daughters — William

JOHN OF MONMOUTH m. Isabel (1248-1256) — Walter — Richard

Alfreda — Joan

THE LANCASTRIAN LORDS OF MONMOUTH

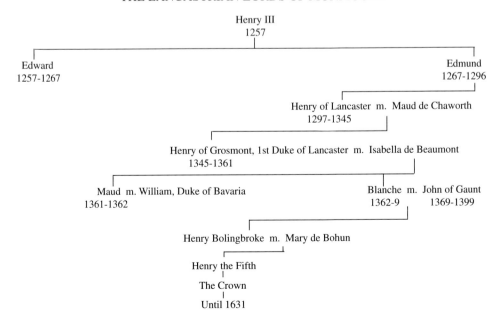

Henry III
1257

Edward
1257-1267

Edmund
1267-1296

Henry of Lancaster m. Maud de Chaworth
1297-1345

Henry of Grosmont, 1st Duke of Lancaster m. Isabella de Beaumont
1345-1361

Maud m. William, Duke of Bavaria
1361-1362

Blanche m. John of Gaunt
1362-9   1369-1399

Henry Bolingbroke m. Mary de Bohun

Henry the Fifth

The Crown

Until 1631

Part Two
THE HOUSE OF LANCASTER 1256 - 1387

1 The Lord Edward

The Lord Edward, later to become Edward I, already held Abergavenny, Skenfrith, Grosmont and White Castle. The addition of Monmouth provided him with a compact and valuable estate whose accounts were audited at his exchequer in Bristol. The Monmouth section shows that enquiries were made 'concerning the heir of Monmouth' by certain officials[1], but the executors sold much of his property, including seed corn and cattle to the Crown.[2] Edward's household expenses in 1256-7 were nearly £8,000 and were paid for out of the profits of his many lordships, Monmouth's contribution being about £200.[3]

These accounts show the intricate details of the economy of the community and, for the first time, the existence of the borough as an important element in its life with its reeve, Gilbert de Lacy, accounting for rents, tolls, chense money and the pleas and perquisites of the hundred court.[4] But the burgesses were troubled and on 3 August 1256 they went before the king at Hereford to find out their position concerning the debts incurred by John of Monmouth.[5] In the presence of the bishop and several Marcher lords, and after paying two gold marks into the Wardrobe, they were granted certain specific rights and assurances.

Firstly, the king confirmed that 'the burgesses and good men of Monmouth' should not be arrested for any debts for which they were not the sureties or principal debtors, 'unless it happen that they be debtors of their commune and dominion'. Secondly, he promised that their goods should not be confiscated on their death, but pass to their heirs, 'without the confiscation of any portion thereof to the king'.

It was not a charter of incorporation, but rather the confirmation of specific privileges which may have been questioned because of John's debts; and partly, a grant of immunity from certain penalties which affected communities without such a charter. Five days later the king granted similar privileges to the citizens of Hereford. Its real significance lies in the emergence of an embryonic corporate body which was important enough to gain an audience with the king, and which had acquired that outward sign of authority and emancipation, a seal. It shows a masted ship as did the seals of many other towns which depended for their supplies on a river, and the words 'Sigill Monemute Commune'.

The minister's accounts throw much light on the economy of the lordship, the manor and the borough. Inevitably their primary concern is with the agriculture on which that economy depended. Crops of wheat, oats, rye, barley, meslin, beans and peas were grown on open fields which at that time were: Chippenham, Castle Field, William's Field and Margaret's or Marret's Field. Dixton Field, which at one time seems to have belonged to the lord had, by 1256, become priory land; while the Warrtrehom (so called from its proximity to the ware tree or gallows) became temporarily attached to Hadnock. A large proportion of each crop was kept for seed, 30 loads of oats out of 125 harvested, and 41 out of 186 loads of wheat.

Ploughmen, the aristocracy of labour, received 5 pence a day and labourers such as weeders, a halfpenny. For one penny they could buy a hen, thirty eggs, a cheese, three gallons of cider, a bridle or a spade. Honey cost 5 pence a gallon, a sack cost 10 pence as did shoeing a horse; goats were 9 pence, wagon wheels 1s 3d, pigs 1s 8d, sparrow hawks 2s, oxen 4s to 5s and horses half a mark. One of the forges was let for 15s 4d and all five mills for a total of £73 and eight hogsheads of wine.

Wine cost 1s 2d a hogshead and, although there was a vineyard at Osbaston, most wine seems to have come through Tintern where it cost twopence a day for storage. It was an even more expensive item to transport, the carriage of fourteen hogsheads from Monmouth to Hereford costing 56s. Movement of goods was sometimes more costly than the movement of men. Carrying twenty-one lampreys from Monmouth to the lord when he was in London cost 81s 6d, while a party consisting of a bailiff, three horsemen and twenty-four footmen spent only 36s on a six-day visit to Cardiff.

Military expenditure was, as always, on quite a different scale, nearly £60 being paid to the reeves of the borough and the manor as 'viewers of the works of the catapults and brattices', and a further 100 marks to the bailiff in the same connection. It is interesting that the borough, as well as the lordship and manor, was involved in these expenses. The castle seems to have employed Welshmen when needed, an item shows 120 footmen of Gwent being paid 52s 6d 'in settlement of their wages'. A crossbow maker received 89s 3d for thirty-four week's work; and in nearby Abergavenny, £12 6s 8d was given to Eynon ap Madoc to equip himself with a 'light horse, a robe, a shield, iron grieves, iron armour and other arms for his need'.[6] Abergavenny also has the stark entry of 3s 'for cutting off three heads'.[7]

The castle was strengthened by the addition in mid-thirteenth century of a round tower similar to those at Skenfrith and Tretower. John Speed in 1610 described it as 'a tower of great height and strength' and shows it on his map standing where Castle House now stands (see map on page 89). That round tower was probably erected by the elder John of Monmouth, and its cost may have accelerated the decline in the family's fortunes. It reinforced the earlier tower, which was in turn supplemented by a new hall, referred to in the next century as 'the Stewards Hall beside the Great Tower'.[8] Stewards were at the head of the administration and important when the lord was so often away from his castle. They were usually English. Out of fifteen medi-aeval stewards of Monmouth, only one, Adam ap Ifor, was Welsh.[9] The appointment was often a reward for service and trust, but when funds were low could be granted to the highest bidder.

The hall had a porch surmounted by a louvre and, because of its use as a courtroom, it survived longer than most other parts of the castle. It had a screens passage at the east end and a staircase connecting it with the great tower. As a further precaution the river crossing to the west seems to have been fortified. This was the Castle Bridge, destroyed in 1233 and replaced by a stone bridge of which a few traces remain. As the castle declined in importance a foot bridge took its place until in the eighteenth century the landlord of the Beaufort Arms built his own bridge (Tibbs Bridge) to lead his visitors to the Pleasure Gardens he laid out on Vauxhall. Amongst his most appreciative guests were John Wesley and Viscount Torrington.

The site of the Castle Bridge, now Tibbs Bridge

Wye Bridge is referred to as Monmouth Bridge in 1282 when it formed one of the boundaries of the Forest of Dean. Originally of wood and possibly north of the present bridge, it was rebuilt, according to Speed, on similar lines to Monnow Bridge which also dates from the end of the thirteenth century.[10]

Monnow Bridge was greatly altered in the nineteenth century when the guard house on the town side was demolished and the road widened.[11] The original stone bridge which supplanted an earlier wooden one[12] dated from the closing years of the thirteenth century. It had a portcullis, machicolis from which missiles could be dropped, and a garderobe discharging into the river.[13]

This bridge linked Monmouth with Overmonnow, sometimes called Little

Top: Monnow Bridge   *Centre:* Wye Bridge   *Bottom:* Clawdd Ddu Bridge

Monmouth, a faubourg or false borough, protected by the Clawdd Ddu or Black Dyke, a form of enlarged barbican or outer defence on the Welsh side. There was an embankment about 5 feet high on the inside of the ditch. The ditch itself is between 35 and 40 feet wide. It may have been possible to flood it from the Monnow, and it is crossed by a small thirteenth century bridge aligned on Monnow Bridge. These defences are very similar to the outer defences of Hereford.[14]

Supplementing the bridges were the gates, of which the most important was the Castle Gate, with its drawbridge over the ditch between the inner and outer bailey. As at Goodrich, it had a garrison chapel nearby. The gaol and the exchequer were housed in that gate and its maintenance caused more concern than any other part of the castle. In 1445 Henry VI ordered that 'a certain tower of our castle of Monmouth where our dearest father of famous memory was born, called "the yatehouse" which is very weak and ruinous' should be rebuilt.[15] In 1550 there was more trouble when the auditors complained that the roof leaked so badly that they had to check the accounts elsewhere. It was at the Castle Gate that transfers of land were made before the chief steward, a rod being passed between the parties to signify the completion of the contract. It was a practice which survived the destruction of the gate in the Civil War and was still occurring in 1775.

The only gate in the outer bailey for which records survive was St. Stephen's Gate in Monnow Street. By 1653, probably as a result of the Civil War, it was known as 'the burnt gate'[16] and by 1705 it had become the town gaol. Outside the gate were steps, and lower down Monnow Street, at Nailers' Lane below the site of the pre-Conquest wooden structure recently discovered, there was another gate with a drawbridge in use during the Civil War.[17]

Edward's tenure of the lordship had been interrupted in 1262 when he exchanged Monmouth and other lands for the Jewry of England.[18] Two years later he was defeated at Lewes and, with his father, became the prisoner of Simon de Montfort. Resistance to Simon was organised in South Wales by Gilbert de Clare and John de Warenne, two magnates who used the Prior of Monmouth as an emissary to the king at Hereford.[19] But Simon, having signed the treaty of Pipton with Llywelyn, captured Monmouth without much difficulty while his ally was ravaging Gwent. He brought the king from Hereford and they were probably in the town at the end of June in 1265. Early in August Simon was killed at Evesham and two years later the honour of Monmouth passed to Edmund Crouchback on his creation as Earl of Lancaster, and for the ensuing centuries, with the Three Castles, it was part of the great Lancastrian estate.[20]

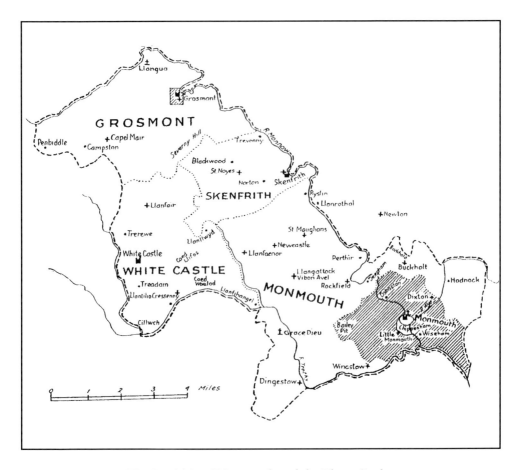

The Lordship of Monmouth and the Three Castles

Edmund gave to the priory the northern part of the Buckholt wood and endowed a lamp in the parish church which was to remain alight for over two hundred years. In 1289 he granted half a mark yearly, out of the rent of a shop near the churchyard, to maintain that lamp and to keep it 'burning day and night in the church of St. Mary before the altar of the Holy Cross in the nave of the parishioners'.[21] The priory church was extended westward to provide for the parishioners in the late twelfth century. It was separated from the monk's church by a stone screen, before which lay the altar of the Holy Cross. The lamp was still burning in 1491, but by 1609 the shop on which it depended had become the church brew house and by the end of the eighteenth century, appropriately enough, the Angel Hotel.[22] The vicar of Monmouth, Richard Stretton, was made responsible for the maintenance of the lamp, and set his seal to the document. The fact that his deputy in this task was the bailiff suggests that wardens had not been appointed in 1289.

The extension of the parish church reduced the need for the large number of small chapels around the town. St. Duellus is not heard of again, nor Garth and Colmanvill, and in 1256 there were anchorites living in St. Thomas's at Overmonnow.[23]

There were still problems in Archenfield, and Llandaff was never reconciled to its loss. In the twelfth century the pope had complained that the Bishop of Hereford allowed excommunicates to be put in communion after the Bishop of Llandaff had pronounced sentence of anathema against them.[24] A hundred years later Henry III reproved the Lord of Monmouth for not doing justice to excommunicates from Llandaff living within the lordship.[25] In many ways the bishops in the March were as jealous of each other's territory as most of the lords.

By the beginning of the fourteenth century the complaints were coming from Hereford. In 1309 a certain Griffin Goht and others broke two doors in St. Mary's and assaulted a man who had fled there for sanctuary. He was dragged out and butchered, his assailants then crossing the Monnow into Llandaff diocese where, so the Bishop of Hereford alleged, no effort was made to bring them to justice. He wrote to his colleague in Llandaff that, 'prelates are bound not only to restrain their people from evil, but also...to correct and punish offenders'. He then asked him to denounce by name the men who by this murder had incurred excommunication.[26]

Where both victim and assailant came from the same diocese, action was usually taken. So that when, in 1318, a fugitive in sanctuary was attacked and the vicar and clerk of Monmouth were injured trying to protect him, the prior, the Dean of Archenfield and the vicars of Dixton and Goodrich, carried out the excommunication, 'having put on the sacred vestments, with cross aloft, bells ringing, candles burning and candles extinguished'.[27] Two years later a quarrel between two priests led to the church itself being polluted by bloodshed. On this occasion the Bishop of Hereford wrote to the

Treasurer of Llandaff, authorising him to enquire into the affair and report to his own bishop, so that he could carry out the reconciliation of the church, in spite of the fact that 'it is recognised as being in our diocese'.[28]

The tradition of sanctuary in the Monnow Valley, where dioceses were separated by a river which was easy to cross, was reinforced by the Templar estates between Garway and Welsh Newton. The Templars had rights of sanctuary on all their lands. It is understandable that four centuries later the Monnow Valley was one of the safest recusant areas in Britain.

During his tenure of the lordship Edmund played his part in local affairs; opposing the Abbot of Tintern's attempts to raise the height of the weirs on the Wye[29]; interceding on behalf of 'the poor men of Monmouth' with the royal treasurer who was making certain demands on them[30]; and repairing the castle with thirty great oaks sent by the king from the Forest of Dean.[31]

According to Walter of Hemingburgh, Edmund was a kindly and generous man, and when, fighting in Gascony in 1296, he found that he could not pay his men, 'his face fell and he sickened about Whitsuntide. So with his failing money his spirits failed also, and after a few days he went the way of all flesh. He ordered our forces to carry him with them and never bury his bones till his debts were paid and this they did'. After a truce they took his bones to his brother, the king, and by him they were given honourable burial in Westminster Abbey.[32] His seal is inscribed 'Eadmundus Filius Regis Anglie Dns Monemut' (Edmund, son of the King of England, lord of Monmouth).

A year after Edmund's death his second son, Henry, did homage before the king 'for the castle, vill and honour of Monmouth...saving the dower of Blanche'. Blanche of Artois was Edmund's second wife and, on her husband's death, most of the Lancastrian lands went to her eldest son Thomas. Henry's inheritance was smaller, but he married Maud de Chaworth and through her obtained lordships in South Wales. Soon after his appointment he interceded with the king to procure a murage grant for the people of Monmouth. These grants, issued in 1297 for five years and renewed in 1315 for three, authorised the bailiff to levy tolls on a long list of imported goods. They included animals, fish, salt, cloth, metals, millstones, firewood and many other items for sale. It was then the responsibility of the townspeople to build the walls.[33](Appendix F)

A glimpse of the way in which Monmouth was divided between the wealthy and the poor can be seen in the Subsidy Rolls for 1292. These show that while the number of persons taxed at over £1 was only fourteen (1.7% of the total) they provided £38 which was 23.6% of the amount collected. Those taxed at over 10s numbered 30 (3.2%) which produced £22 (16.6% of the total). Those taxed at over 5s, ninety-seven in all (or 12.2%), produced £38 (23.6% of the total) while the 635 taxed below 5s (82.4%) produced £63 (32.6% of the total). The top forty-four persons in all produced £60 and the bottom 750 produced £101. Seemingly it was a reasonably fair system of taxation since there were many who did not appear on the subsidy roll because they did not own enough property.[34]

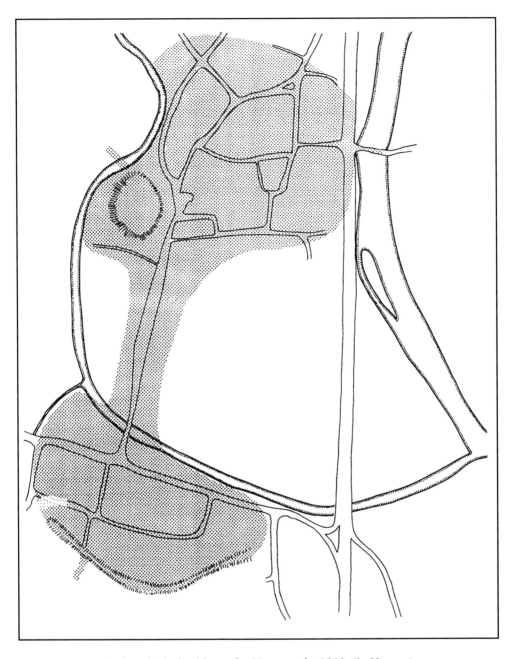

Archaeological evidence for Monmouth c1300. (L. Harper)

ERRATUM : Page 54, paragraph 5, line 7 :
635 to read 653

So this taxed community of just under 800 persons had then to set about building the town walls using, presumably, the untaxed citizens to do the work. Their construction was slow and disruptive. The walls were designed to deter not only aggressors, but undesirables, vagrants and thieves and, once completed, were an economic status symbol and a mark of civic importance.

It is not clear how far this ambitious enterprise got but Leland, writing in the first half of the sixteenth century, described Monmouth as 'enclosed by a wall on that part which is not defended by rivers...but now through age, the wall is broken and much of the defence is down. Nevertheless extensive ruins remain along with a deep ditch'. Most of these ruins were removed in the eighteenth century when the citizens discovered the profitable market for the 'cinders' on which their foundations rested.

The gates outlasted the town walls: Monks' Gate, on the road from the priory to the priory farm, was pulled down in 1710[35]; it probably stood near the ditch discovered below Singleton House; Dixton Gate was removed in 1770 because it hindered the passage of coaches, but one of the towers is incorporated in the Nag's Head Inn; Wye Gate has gone completely.

Chippenham Gate does not appear to have been part of the defensive system but the place where tolls were collected from graziers using Chippenham after the hay had been cut. The town walls seem to have been constructed mainly between 1296 and 1320 and reflect the importance Monmouth was acquiring as a Lancastrian stronghold, closely linked to the king, in the usually unstable March.

This was shown by the increased demand for armed forces for service further afield. In 1298 Henry was commissioned to array 300 Welsh footmen for the Scottish expedition[36] and he served in the King's Division at Falkirk, a victory which owed much to the skill with which the Welsh used their bows and slings. Three hundred men was the usual requirement from this district and it was repeated in 1322[37]. The footmen were paid 4d a day and had defensive armour but the Monmouth contingent was not always of high quality. In 1316 the bailiff was accused of producing 'worthless rascals'[38] because he took money to leave the good men at home.

During the closing years of the thirteenth century St. Briavels became an important source of crossbow bolts. During Edward I's wars against Wales he acquired many thousands from this area. Iron arrow heads were also being made at the Overmonnow forges in the late thirteenth century.

Henry, like his father, was involved in a continuing series of disputes over the correct use of the river Wye. For Monmouth, which was trying to improve its defences by murage tolls on every import from wine to stockfish, it was essential to have free passage for shipping from Chepstow and Bristol.

It was less important that the river should remain navigable upstream, but it was over this stretch that difficulties were first encountered by Hereford. As a result a commission was appointed in 1301 to enquire into 'the weirs, dykes and stakes in the water of Wye between Hereford and Monmouth, as it appears that boats cannot pass as they were wont'[39]. The jury was to be appointed jointly by the Sheriff of Hereford and Henry of Lancaster but its deliberations were unproductive.

Thirty years later Henry was still complaining of 'losses to him and his town of Monmouth by obstruction of the river Wye' at Tintern where the abbot had raised various weirs by as much as 6 feet.[40] An inquisition denied the abbot's right to do this and the Sheriff of Gloucester was ordered to see that they were lowered. He, in turn, sent the Bailiff of St. Briavels to carry out the demolition, but the bailiff was set upon by the abbot and his monks as he began work.

The abbot then complained that Henry had taken the law into his own hands, pulled down Ithel's weir and Ashweir and intended to destroy the rest. He pointed out that all these weirs lay in the liberty of Chepstow which belonged to the king's uncle.[41] As a result yet another commission was appointed to find out whether the weirs were in Wales or Gloucestershire. Henry countered the abbot's complaints with his own, that 'boats and ships with wine and victuals and other lading could not cross to the earl's town of Monmouth and to other places adjacent, to the danger of the earl and of all men who so wished to cross'.

The fiercest disputes were usually over the lower Wye, the meanders between Monmouth and Hereford making it quicker to use pack horses. Thus in 1296 the Countess of Pembroke received a barrel of venison at Goodrich Castle which had come from Bristol to Monmouth by boat and then overland, the whole journey taking seven days. Quarrels over the use of the river were endemic.

Henry was also involved in conflict with the prior and burgesses of Monmouth. With the former the trouble was over the right of monastic tenants to grind their corn at the priory mill, the monks complaining that Henry's bailiffs were amercing those who wished to grind there.[42] A compromise was reached and Henry ordered his officials to allow the monks free use of the lord's mills which was not, of course, what they wanted. The quarrel with the burgesses was over their duty to keep watch and ward, an obligation to which they had become liable by the statute of Winchester in 1285. In 1308 the two parties met in Monmouth. The burgesses agreed to keep watch from the feast of the Holy Cross in May until the fairs of St. Martin and St. Bartholomew, in time of war and at any other time when summoned by the lord. They admitted refusing to perform some of these duties 'and other trespasses' and agreed in expiation to owe the lord 20 marks which should be payable on demand. In witness the men of the commonalty affixed their seal.[43]

The burgesses as a corporate body, accumulated power and privilege as the authority and prestige of the priory declined. This decline was due partly to financial difficulties, and partly to a deterioration in the quality of the men living there. The prior at the beginning of the fourteenth century was typical; a monk from Saumur called David, approved by the Bishop of Hereford as 'a man prudent and honest in matters spiritual and temporal, circumspect and sufficiently educated'.[44] But two years later David's goods were sequestrated and the sequestration was not lifted until he had paid the king '£62:0:10 which he owes us of his many debts'.[45]

A Prior of Monmouth was usually chosen by the Abbot of Saumur from amongst his monks. His appointment was then confirmed by the Bishop of Hereford who instituted him to the office, but the actual induction was often carried out by a local vicar. Thus David, the prior in question, was inducted by the Vicar of Dixton.[46] Thirteen years later David appointed one of his own monks to be Vicar of Dixton.[47] Similarly he appointed the next Vicar of Monmouth[48] who, in turn, inducted David's successor to the priory.[49]

The right of priors to appoint vicars to their appropriated churches was jealously guarded. Most of these vicars received the lesser tithes or a small salary, not to be less than five marks, 'except in those part of Wales, where on account of the slenderness of the churches, vicars are content with a smaller stipend'.[50] The prior, as rector, was responsible for the maintenance of the chancel of an appropriated church; the vicar and his parishioners for the nave, the vestments and the furniture. Once installed, the vicar was difficult to dislodge. This security of tenure gave him a position of influence which tended to increase as the authority of the priory declined. His duties were clearly laid down by Bishop Cantilupe of Hereford: to administer the sacraments, to hear confession, and to teach the Ten Commandments, the Seven Sins, the Seven Sacraments, and the Creed.[51]

Henry, Lord of Monmouth had carried the royal sceptre, surmounted by a dove, at the coronation of Edward II. Nineteen years later he was present in Monmouth Castle when the same king was forced to hand over the great seal of England to his captors. In the interval he had survived the taint of his brother's execution for treason at Pontefract and, by political moderation, had become Earl of Lancaster in 1324. When the captive king was brought to Monmouth two years later he was met by an enemy, Bishop Orleton of Hereford, who demanded the royal seal.[52] Edward refused and gave it to his messenger, Edward Blount, remarking that his consort and son might have it and do with it as they liked. Six days later it was given to the queen at Much Marcle and on that day the king set out once more on the tragic journey that was to end in horror at Berkeley Castle.

Henry of Lancaster was also prominent at the coronation of Edward III, girding the king with the sword of knighthood; but by 1330 he was nearly blind and three years later he handed over the administration of Monmouth and the Three Castles to his brilliant son, Henry of Grosmont.

Variously known as Henry the Wrynecked, Earl of Lancaster, Earl of Derby and finally as Duke of Lancaster, he was born at Grosmont in 1299 and was the only surviving son of Henry and Maud de Chaworth. His first important appointment was as Captain-General of the English forces in Scotland. Thereafter, as commander on sea or land, diplomat, statesman, royal advisor and as the writer of what has been described as the masterpiece of French prose in fourteenth century England, his services were unsurpassed.

Henry of Grosmont, born in Grosmont Castle in 1299, was made Duke of Lancaster in 1351. He was a distinguished soldier and fought in the earlier part of the Hundred Years War in France. Grosmont appears to have been one of his favourite residences. This illustration comes from the fifteenth century Bruges Garter Book (By kind permission of the British Library, Stowe Ms.594, f.8).

3 Henry of Grosmont (Duke of Lancaster)

In the year that his father died (1345) Henry, who was already Earl of Derby, assumed command, as Earl of Lancaster, of Edward's expedition to Gascony. It was there, while the king and the Black Prince were fighting at Crecy, that Henry gained his reputation for chivalry, anticipating the Black Prince's feasting of defeated enemies, by entertaining his own captives to a banquet after the battle of Auberoche. From the profits of this campaign Henry built his palace of the Savoy. His hospitality was such that on a visit to the Pope at Avignon it was said of him, 'There is no one like him in the world'.

In 1350, crying 'Derby to the rescue', he saved the lives of the Black Prince and John of Gaunt in a sea battle off Winchester. In the following year he became the first Duke of Lancaster. He was already a founder member of the order of the Garter, and was preceded as an English duke only by the Black Prince. His arms were, scarlet, three gold leopards passant for England, with a blue label of France with three gold fleurs de lis on each of its three points to show that he was a cadet of the royal house. In the last year of his life he was styled 'Duke of Lancaster, Earl of Derby, Lincoln and Leicester, Steward of England, Lord of Bergerac and Beaufort'. He held twenty-three castles in England and Wales. From his estates on the English side of the Channel alone, he had an income of £8,380.[53]

He died on 23 March 1361, a victim of the Second Pestilence, and was buried at Leicester, mourned and honoured by the greatest in the land. 'He outstripped all in deeds and renown' wrote the chronicler, Jean le Bel. He left two daughters and, more important, a remarkable book, *Le Livre de Seyntz Medicines*, written in 1354 by 'the crazy miserable sinner ERTSACNAL ED CUD IRNEH', his name written backwards in surviving manuscripts.

It is an allegory. As a man needs a physician to cure his wounds, so does mankind. The only physician who can cure the world's wounds, through which the seven deadly sins enter, is Christ - 'Tresdouze Sire' as Henry calls Him. The book is full of vivid observations and practical advice. As a great jouster himself, Henry compares Christ's battles for mankind with those of a knight in the lists, and as an enthusiastic huntsman he described three ways of getting rid of foxes, and likens them to the three ways of removing sin, which stinks like a fox, from a man's body.[54]

Unlike most other devotional books of this century, *Le Livre de Seyntz Medicines* is not the work of a theologian but of a busy man of the world, and is all the more impressive for that. It contains much information about life in general such as making capon broth by cooking without fire. That system of a small pot containing the food, placed inside a larger one and the space between filled with unslaked lime provided enough heat for slow cooking, giving a man time to walk between 'five and seven leagues'. One of the first known examples of such pots was excavated at 69 Monnow Street in 1988 by the Monmouth Archaeological Society.

It would not have been surprising if a man as fully occupied as Henry of

Une chofe q̄ moelt reconforte une fieble defheites, fi eſt q̄ homme preigne un chapon ⁊ l'en mette en une petite potte de terre, ⁊ cette potte eſt ſi forte eſopee q̄ rienſ ne poet entrer ne iſſir; ⁊ puis le pent homme en un autre veſſel pleyn de eawe ſur le freu ⁊ le quit homme tantqe il ſoit pluſ q̄ quit; ⁊ la ſuour q̄ vient ſi prent homme ⁊ le done a malade, ⁊ ſi chofe de grande ſuſt-ence.

The recipe for cooking capons without fire from *Le Livre de Seyntz Medicines*.

Pots for cooking without fire excavated from a house in Monnow Street. The site was being rebuilt in the thirteenth century. *(By permission of Monmouth Archaeological Society)*

Grosmont had left no mark on Monmouth. He spent most of his life at court or abroad and three years after his father's death England had been swept by the Black Death. Yet during his tenure of the lordship the castle of Monmouth was rebuilt in princely style, as was the church tower, while the community of which they were the centre gained a coherence and stature which it had rarely known before and which, after the rebellion of Glyn Dwr at the beginning of the next century, it was seldom to know again.

The west wall of the fourteenth century tower of St. Mary's church.

Monmouth Castle with its chancery, exchequer and judiciary was held of the king by the service of fifteen knights' fees. The whole lordship was further sub-divided into military fiefs, held by English or Welsh knights in return for military service, which involved the provision for forty days of a fully armed knight with barded horse when the lord required. These sub-lordships were empowered to sub-let in return for service, and so smaller fiefs were created in each estate. The site of a typical one which consisted of a moated hall can be seen at Dixton. It is referred to as the hall of the Lord of Dixton in a survey of the boundaries in 1432. These smaller lords were really squires. An early one was Robert Bruht, who held at his death at Dixton in 1327, a house and garden, 100 acres of arable, 2 acres of meadow, 3 acres of forest, half a water-mill on Mallybrook, a dovecot and 42s 3d in rent. He owed homage by the service of half a knight's fee and the finding of one man to follow his lord to war.[55]

Centred on the castle was the manorial demesne, with its Barton in the outer bailey, its subordinate granges and open fields. The Barton, originally a barn for collecting produce, lay behind Church Street, the grange was in St. James Street and was referred to as the Lord's Barn in later documents.[56] Dependant and interwoven were the lands of the customary tenants, the free tenants and the cottars. Before the Black Death the size of the demesne based on the Barton in Monmouth was about 300 acres, while that based on Hadnock was about 400. The monks too held extensive lands, controlled with lay assistance from the Priory Farm. The borough as yet held little land.

Lastly there were the parishes, acquiring an influence, authority and wealth of their own. They had to be self-supporting, so their size depended on the quality of the land and the ease with which it could be worked. This meant that the better the land, the smaller the parish. Dixton was more extensive than Monmouth because so much of its land was high woodland. From the fourteenth century onwards the parishes rather than the priory began to dominate the religious life of the community.

The decline in the fortunes of the priory was partly financial, partly due to the tendency for abler men to prefer the university to the cloister, and partly to the Hundred Years War severing the alien priories from their parent abbeys in France. Financial difficulties went back to the thirteenth century. As early as 1254 there had been trouble over the responsibility for paying the charges on the parishes.[57] Property had been sold to meet the demands of taxation and, in 1264, Gilbert Moretau, an able administrator, was sent from Saumur to manage affairs.[58] He revoked all alienation of monastic land and curtailed the indiscriminate granting of pensions, a recurrent source of financial embarrassment.

At the outbreak of the Hundred Years War the priory was severed from the parent abbey at Saumur, and the right of presentation to all appropriated churches passed, along with the yearly apport, to the Crown. The right of presentation was in dispute before the outbreak of war, especially at Goodrich, which in 1331 had two vicars appointed simultaneously by the lord and prior.[59] The argument dragged on until 1524 when the prior recovered his rights, only to sell them to a layman.[60]

Pestilence affected the Monmouth area in 1349, 1361 and 1369. The first outbreak, the Black Death, was probably brought by boat from Bristol. It caused inevitable upheaval among the parochial clergy as the churches, to which the terrified people flocked, became a primary source of infection. The resulting dislocation can be gathered by consulting almost any list of vicars in any church porch, or more comprehensively in the diocesan registers.

In 1349 at least 176 priests were instituted in the diocese of Hereford, compared with five in 1345, six in 1346, six in 1347 and ten in 1348. Not all of the 176 vacancies were caused by death but in the first seven months of the year fifty were.[61] St. Mary's had a new vicar on 26 July[62] who was replaced ten months later[63], while at Dixton there were three; William (an alien), Ralph Gosenlinch and William Morel.[64] William was cited in 1346 when Edward III, on the outbreak of war, ordered all bishops to submit the names of any aliens living in their diocese. Hereford named two, but as William was too old and feeble to be a danger to the state, he was allowed to remain at Dixton until he died in January 1349.[65] His successor Ralph Gosenlinch also died; William Morel survived.

Just as the Black Death disorganised the parishes, so it created difficulties in the manor. This was largely because the outbreak in 1348/9 was followed by a second in 1361 and a third in 1369. These later visitations undid any reorganisation that might have been carried out after 1349, with the result that the lords were compelled to cut their losses and keep the land in cultivation by farming it out to lessees. By 1353 the whole demesne of Monmouth, amounting to 243 acres, had been let for twelve years to three men who paid 1s 1d an acre and received all instruments, ploughs and wagons necessary for working the land.[66] These were the first steps in the conversion of the feudal manor to the modern estate. The three beneficiaries were Lawrence Greyndor, John de la Rye and John Tyler.

The first of these came from Hadnock and in 1353 had a son John. He became a retainer of John of Gaunt to whom in 1392 he granted Hadnock. Then, having been given an annuity of 20 marks by Henry IV, he progressed to be MP for the county of Hereford in 1401 and 1404, and Sheriff of Gloucester in 1405, 1411 and 1414. 'Valiant for King Hal', he served with Henry IV in Scotland, fought at the Battle of Shrewsbury in 1403 and helped in the defeat of Glyn Dwr at Grosmont in 1405. He was in charge of Monmouth, Skenfrith and Grosmont castles in 1405/6 and in the king's retinue at Agincourt. He is a good example of the way an able soldier of fairly humble origin could rise rapidly once favoured by the crown.[67]

Monmouth was particularly affected by the First and Third Pestilences, but not to any extent by the Second in which Henry of Grosmont died.[68] In 1370 the minister's accounts show many entries dealing with the plague; increased rents, lands in decay, payments in arrear, oxen in bad condition, mills let to farm, and land valued at over £12 'in the hands of the lord through lack of tenants caused both by the first Pestilence as well as the pestilence happening in the year 43 [1369]'.[69]

The duties of customary tenants were such a mixture of feudal obligation and Welsh custom that they are worth considering in detail. A typical Welsh tenant of the fee of Hadnock, David ap David held a messuage and 31 acres in Rockfield, in return for the following services:[70]

$7\frac{3}{4}$ d at the term of St. Dudra, and 3d at Michaelmas, and of kilth $7\frac{3}{4}$ d

Kilth, or Cylch, was a Welsh tribal due owed when the king visited a district to administer justice. It first consisted of hospitality and food, but was later commuted to a fixed money charge. The Welsh word means circuit and in Monmouth it was still being paid in 1492.

and 1 hen at Christmas

Sometimes referred to as woodhens, they were paid to the lord in return for the right to gather firewood. The custom may, together with the difficulty of keeping stock alive through the winter, have been the origin of the Christmas dinner.

and he ought to harrow for 3 days
and he ought to plough for $3\frac{1}{2}$ days
and he ought to fork hay for $1\frac{1}{2}$ days
and he ought to reap the lord's corn for $3\frac{1}{2}$ days.

Ploughing and harrowing services sometimes depended on the possession of an ox. Thus at Worthybrook, one of the sub-manors, customary tenants 'plough with an ox, and if they have no ox, they give nothing'.

and to carry 2 loads of wood from Coytboghan to Monmouth Castle before Christmas...and if he has no horse for carrying wood to the said castle, he is to find a man to cut wood there.

Carrying wood to the castle was one of the Welsh hauling services. It depended on ownership of a horse and for this reason was known as Averagium from affer, a horse.

and to clean the mill pond at Newmill

David ap David lived at Rockfield and the New Mill is on the Monnow in that neighbourhood.

and to watch a thief if one shall fly to the church

Watching a thief in sanctuary was a Welsh obligation which was enforced to prevent the refugee escaping or procuring food before his crime was investigated. At Worthybrook it was more specific: 'If anyone happen to flee for any felony to the church and acknowledges his felony, then he [each villein] ought to keep the felon with his neighbours of the same township, one night'.[71] The watcher had a double duty; to see that the felon left after 24 hours, and at the same time prevent the victims trying to drag him from the church.

and he owes suit of court

Courts were assemblies where orders were issued and justice debated. An essential element of these courts was the suitor whose knowledge of local affairs and customs, largely unwritten, was essential. They were not jurors but advisors to the steward. Failure to attend might lead to punishment. In 1308 a burgess of Monmouth paid 20 marks to recover the lord's goodwill at one such court.[72]

and suit of mill

This was one of the most jealously guarded of the lord's privileges and was reinforced with heavy penalties on anyone using a hand quern. A portion of corn when the mill was used was taken as toll. Only the tenants of the priory were excused payment. The obligation was always resented but as late as 1561, after a dispute with the queen, a commission decided that tenants ought to grind their corn at her mills. Later still, in 1696, when the Earl of Worcester as lord brought an action against several of his tenants for not grinding in his mill, the common council took upon itself to defend the suit at its own expense. Mills were essential to every community and were, as a result, early targets in any Welsh rebellion.

and he owes leir and merchiet for his daughters

Leir or Leyrwyt was a fine for incontinence on the part of the tenant's daughters. Pregnancy deprived the lord of the girls' services for a time and the father paid the fine in recompense. Merchiet was a similar fine paid by the father when his daughter wished to get married. Again the reasoning was that, when married, she would not be able to give as much service as she did when single.

and he shall pay tak for his hogs, namely for unringed pigs 1d and for Hoggs $\frac{1}{2}$d

Tak, wormtak or wrintak was a payment exacted by the lord when his woods were used in autumn to feed the tenants' swine. It was allied to Pannage, by which tenants could put their pigs in the forest to eat the beech mast and acorns, but differed from it in being compulsory. In 1370 tak produced 5s 6d in Monmouth.

and he ought to hunt in Hodenak wood with the lord and other royalty services.

The hunting at Hadnock consisted of acting as a beater. The wood was originally part of the Forest of Dean but King John gave John of Monmouth permission to enclose it and make a park. By the end of the century the chase of Hadnock was outside the forest.

The size of David ap David's holding was more typical of England than Wales. Thirty acres was about the average holding of an English customary tenant, whereas in Wales it was frequently less than 10 acres. This small holding at Rockfield is a good example of the compromise which emerged from the confrontation of Marcher law and Welsh custom.

4 John of Gaunt

When Henry of Grosmont died he left his estates to his daughters, Maud of Bavaria, who received Monmouth, and Blanche, who had married John of Gaunt at the age of 12. Maud returned from abroad to take up her inheritance, but died on Palm Sunday in 1362 leaving her inheritance to John of Gaunt.[73] There were rumours that she had been poisoned but little evidence to support them. But Blanche, like her sister, died young and on her death her great fortune passed to her husband who had been created Duke of Lancaster in 1362, when the king, at Westminster, girded him with a sword and placed a fur cap on his head encircled with a ring of pearls and gold.

Blanche was a patron of Geoffrey Chaucer who dedicated his *Book of the Duchess* to her. It contains a long description of her beauty and grace:

> And good faire WHYTE she hete.
> That was my lady's name right
> She was bothe fair and bright.
> She hadde not hire name wrong.
> Right faire shuldres, and body long
> She hadde, and armes every lith
> Fattish, flesshy, not greet therewith;
> Right whyte handes, and nayles red,
> Round brestes, and of good brede
> Her hippes were, a streight flat bak.

A more affectionate description of her was Froissart's:

> Help! put a plaster
> On my heart...I am so full of melancholy
> She was young and pretty when she died,
> About twenty-two years old.
> Gay, joyous, frolicsome, frisky
> Sweet, simple, modest of mien
> The excellent lady was called Blanche.

These are the most detailed descriptions we have of the wife of any early Lord of Monmouth. She left a son, the infant Henry, who was to become the fourth king of that name in England.

The last years of Edward III were years of dissension. On the one hand was the Black Prince, a dying man, and on the other, John of Gaunt, none too honest or successful, by no means 'time-honoured' yet. The Black Prince died in 1376 and the king one year later. This left the country to the 10 years old Richard of Bordeaux and the overwhelming influence of John of Gaunt. Monmouth was one of John of Gaunt's favourite castles. Here he entertained his mother, Queen Philippa, in what by 1370 was known as the Queen's Chamber. Evidence of the social importance of Monmouth at this time is shown by the fine imported Venetian glass excavated by local archaeologists in Monnow Street.

The minister's accounts for 1370 contain several items dealing with repairs to the castle, including the re-tiling of the Queen's Chamber and the chapel near the gate. Tilers were paid 4d a day. The repair of two windows in the chapel cost 13s 4d, which included the wages of the glaziers and the cost of the glass, while a new gallows for hanging robbers cost 1s 6d. The castle garden was in existence and the grass and the produce earned 4s. The tithe on that was 4d.[74] Stored in the castle were the goods of the dead, probably plague victims. They included a table worth 8d, a carpet, pewter chargers and candlesticks, each valued at 1s and a crowder worth 2s. The crowder or crwth, a stringed musical instrument, is the root of a group of common Monmouth surnames; Crowden, Crowther and Croudace.

The reorganisation of the castle would have been the responsibility of the steward, John Sergeant, who was also steward of the castle at Abergavenny. He was assisted by one of the first Welshmen to hold important administrative office at the castle, John ap Gwilym, a man who had raised himself to become receiver in 1399.[75] He was also receiver of Chepstow and Usk. The lordship at this time was divided into eight manors: Wyesham, Dixton, Cunstone (Llangunville), Perthir, Newcastle, Rockfield, Dingestow and Holywell.

Although the castle flourished, all was not well at the priory. The prior was still admitting burgesses but the buildings and the church were in need of funds. To raise money an indulgence was granted by the Pope to all those giving alms to the church 'in which are the relics of the Holy Cross, the Sepulchre, Winding Sheet, and other garments of Our Lord, as well as of many saints'.[76]

The castle chapel was still in use and the chantry there had been granted by the Duke of Lancaster to Grace Dieu in 1357 when the accounts of the manor show an item of bread, wine and candles for the castle chapel.

Amongst the church's benefactors was Richard Mylton who left money for a pair of vestments in 1393.[77] His will is of interest because it shows something of the contents of a wealthy man's library and, at the same time, the growing number and variety of the parochial clergy. After commending his soul to God, and his body to the Church of the Blessed Mary of Monmouth, the will continued:

I bequeath to the High Altar for forgotten tenths, One Summa Summarum[78] and one Avicenna on the canon[79], or the value thereof for the purchase of a pair of vestments.

Gifts for forgotten tenths were encouraged by the reading in church, four times a year, of the Greater Excommunication.

I bequeath to Sir Roger Monke, parish chaplain at the same place, one Galfridus on the Summa;
To Sir Thomas Donche my Pars Oculi.[80]
To Master John Bryde the Sixth Book with Glossary.

To Brother John Lodelawe the Oculis Moralis cum dicta salutis
To Brother Thomas Donne a Legenda Aurea.[81]
To Stephen Cooke one Senapio.

Mylton then confirmed the gifts of land, tenements and burgages which he had already made to his private chaplain, Nicholas; and the residue to his wife. He appointed Nicholas to be his executor, 'under the supervision of Robert Huntley', and ordered him to dispose of all debts still due, 'for my soul, and my wife's soul, and the souls of the faithful departed'.

The will assumed prominence because it led to a protracted quarrel between the Bishop of Hereford and the Archbishop of Canterbury. Its local interest lay in the beneficiaries. David Howell, vicar of Monmouth at the time, got nothing, probably deservedly, but Roger Monke, the parish chaplain, received a book and acted as a witness.[82] Robert Huntley, the supervisor of the executor was the ancestor of Hugh Huntley of Hadnock who was to become receiver of many castles, Chancellor of Monmouth in 1479 and eventually Justiciar of South Wales.[83] He died in 1501 and asked in his will to be buried at Dixton Church, leaving bequests to the vicar and the Hospital of St. Nicholas there. Other bequests went to monks, friars and his own private chaplain. Amongst the witnesses was the parish clerk, John Ferrour, who was to die as vicar of Monmouth in 1408.

The appointment of an executor 'under supervision' illustrates the mediaeval distrust of executors, a distrust which one of the surviving tiles in St Mary's church expresses in doggerel:

Thenke mon thi liffe	Think man.
Mai not eu endure	Thy life will not last forever
That thou dost thiself	Of what you do yourself
Of that thou art sure	you can be sure.
But that thou kepist	But what you leave to
Unto thi sector cure	your executor to do,
And eu hit availe thee	it is luck if it is
Hit is but aventure.[84]	of any benefit.

The fourteenth century has been called the age of the devout layman, and Richard Mylton's will gives some substance to the claim. There were others not so devout. The parish's seamier side was uncovered by Bishop Trefnant of Hereford on a visitation in 1397.[85] The parishioners claimed that matins and vespers were not being said, that the vicar was absent at the Roman Curia and that there was no one to take his place. They reported that the vicarage house was level with the ground and that, apart from the monks, there was no one to minister to the sick at night or to give extreme unction.

At Overmonnow the chancel roof was defective, while at Dixton the parishioners complained that it was so dark, even in the middle of the morning, that the church had to be continually lit by candles. In Monmouth, Roger

Monke, the parish chaplain who had benefited from Richard Mylton's will, was accused of buying and selling goods at a profit; a large number of parishioners were said to practice their crafts on the Lord's Day; and one man refused even to receive the Lord's bread. There follows a list of those living in sin in the parish, those who had made clandestine marriages and the name of the keeper of the town brothel.

Other documents from the same decade confirm that all was not well. A certain Welshman was 'counterfeiting groats, pence and halfpence with flanders plate and quicksilver...also clipping money, to wit, groats and half groats of silver, and nobles of gold'.[86] He was pardoned as was John Cook, twice in one year, for stealing animals.[87] So was Roger Dyear for all felonies committed by him except murders, treasons and rapes.[88] This seems to have been misplaced clemency as two years later he managed to escape from the King's prison at Worcester.

It was a century of great national disasters, of plague, rebellion and war. Even so the value of the lordship remained fairly stable: in 1331 £514, in 1332 £619, between 1386 and 1391 £517, and in 1395 £509.[89] The money thus being made from various sources was one of the contributory causes of the Welsh rebellion. But in the closing years of the fourteenth century a child was born in Monmouth castle who was to bring glory to the country and royal recognition to the town.

REFERENCES Part Two

(Abbreviations for some of the more frequently cited sources appear on page 8)

[1]   SWMRS No. 4, 1957, p.29.
[2]   Ibid., p.15. 128 oxen bought for £25 12s 0d and winter seed corn for £30.
[3]   N. Denholm-Young, *Seignorial Administration in England*, p.9.
[4]   SWMRS, chence money was for a licence to trade.
[5]   P.R.O. C 146/9843. See Appendix E.
[6]   SWMRS no. 3, 1954, p.45.
[7]   'in tribus capitibus amputandis'
[8]   P.R.O. DL 29/594/9506.
[9]   R. R. Davies, *Lordship and Society in the March of Wales, 1282 - 1400*, p.207.
[10] MBA. CM 29/11/1703 which states, 'the new bridge adjoining the Great Bridge over Wye to be finished at speed'.
[11] MBA. CM R & V. 5/7/1819.
[12] The timbers have been dated to the middle of the twelfth century.
[13] M. L. J. Rowlands, *Monnow Bridge and Gate*. Sutton, 1994.
[14] Sir Cyril Fox, *Offa's Dyke*, 1955, p.182. Clawdd Du ramparts were excavated by M.A.S. in 1966. *Archaeology in Wales*, 1991.
[15] P.R.O. DL 37/12 6d.
[16] MBA. C 1653.
[17] In 1896 in a paper on the fortifications of Monmouth Mrs. Bagnall Oakeley wrote, 'the recent discovery of the old wall further down Monnow Street ex plains this gate'. A hundred years later the discovery of a large wooden struc ture near this site raises questions. See Clarke, 'Evidence for a Pre-Norman structure at Monmouth', M.A. XII, 1996.
[18] Cal. Patent Rolls, 1258-1266, p.233.
[19] Ibid., p.248.

[20] P.R.O. DL 10/109.

[21] P.R.O. DL 42/1, fo. 20.

[22] As late as 1926 a receipt was made out for 'The Church Brew House now Angel Hotel'. MBA. PM 1926.

[23] SWMRS no. 4, p.17.

[24] J. Conway Davies, *Episcopal Acts Relating to Welsh Dioceses*, vol. 2, p.629.

[25] Cal. Close Rolls 1251-1253, p.226.

[26] Regist. R. Swinfield, pp.446-448.

[27] Regist. A. Orleton, p.63.

[28] Ibid., p.157.

[29] Cal. Patent Rolls 1272-1281, p.408.

[30] Cal. Ancient Correspondence concerning Wales, p. 213.

[31] Cal. Close Rolls Edward I, p. 79.

[32] Walter of Heminburgh, *Chronicon II*, pp.72-74.

[33] P.R.O. C 66/117. Appendix F.

[34] R. R. Davies, op. cit., p.400.

[35] MBA. CM 29/2/1709. This gave permission for it to be taken down.

[36] Cal. Patent Rolls, 1292-1301, p.343.

[37] Ibid., 14/2/1322.

[38] Cal. Chancery Warrants, p.437.

[39] Cal. Patent Rolls, 1292-1301, p.627.

[40] Ibid., 1330-1334, p.201. The weirs in question were Bigsweir, Ithelsweir and Ashweir, all of which had to be lowered by 6 feet; and Walweir, Plumweir, Stanweir, Batyngweir and Brockweir which were 5 feet too high.

[41] Cal. Close Rolls, Edward III, p.304.

[42] Cal. Ancient Correspondence concerning Wales, p.214.

[43] MBA. Transcription marked DL fo. 18., no. 8. Gt. Cowcher.

[44] Regist. R. Swinfield, p.376.

[45] Ibid., p.442.

[46] Ibid., p.376.

[47] Ibid., p.542.

[48] Ibid., p.537.

[49] Ibid., p.500.

[50] E. T. Davies, *Ecclesiastical History of Monmouthshire*, p.103.

[51] Wilkins Concilia I, p.665.

[52] Regist. Orleton, Introduction, p. xxxvii.

[53] K. Fowler, *The King's Lieutenant*, 1969, p.172. Grosmont Castle, famous for its deer park, was a favourite Lancastrian residence.

[54] W. A. Pantin, *The English Church in the Fourteenth Century*, pp.231-233.

[55] DL 42/1 fo. 21. (1327).

[56] A site close to the Grange was recently excavated by M.A.S. and revealed crucible sherds for metal working, a splendid fireback with the arms of Elizabeth I and a fine selection of pottery. See *Archaeology in Wales*, vol. 34, 1994.

[57] P.R.O. Ancient Deeds. Court of Augmentation No. B 8813.

[58] Paul Marchegay, 'Les Prieurés Anglais de Saint Florent près Saumur', p.190. There is a microfilm of most of the charters in MBA.

[59] Regist. T. Charlton, pp.13, 55. There was similar trouble at Staunton.

[60] Regist. C. Booth, p.184.

[61] Regist. J. de Trillek, pp.374-378.

[62] Ibid., p.378.

[63] Ibid., p.382.

[64] Ibid., p.393.

[65] Ibid., p.261.

[66] P.R.O. DL 29/594/9506.

[67] R. A. Griffiths, *The Principality of Wales in the Later Middle Ages*, 1972.

68   In the year of the Second Pestilence (1361) the profits of the Borough were £61 13s 0d, made up of £6 13s 0d in rents, £25 in tolls, £15 from profits of justice and £15 from other items (P.R.O. C 135/161).

69   P.R.O. DL 29/594/9506.

70   P.R.O. Rentals and Surveys, fo. 13/7.

71   Quoted by W. Rees, *South Wales and the March*, p.60.

72   DL 42/1, fo.18.

73   Kington: Chronicon. Rolls Series, no. 92, II, p.116.

74   P.R.O. DL 29/594/9506. The castle garden, recently recreated, attempts to show only plants which could have been known to Henry V. They include culinary herbs like Lovage, wound herbs like Solomon's Seal, aphrodisiacs like Lady's Mantle, and plants such as Hyssop and Lavender to counteract the stench of latrines and cesspits.

75   R. R. Davies, op. cit., 204/5.

76   Cal. of Papal Registers: (papal Letters), V, p.258.

77   Regist. P. Trefnant, p.100.

78   The *Summa Summarum*, written c1326 by William of Pagula, was a comprehensive work on canon law and theology, dealing with every problem likely to affect the fourteenth century ecclesiastic.

79   Avicenna (980-1037) wrote many books in his native Persian, amongst which his Canon of Medicine was, for long, a fundamental work in the west.

80   The Pars Oculi, the first part of the Oculis Sacerdotus, written c. 1327, was a manual of instruction on confession for a priest to pass on to his parishioners.

81   The Bishop of Hereford's copy of the Golden Legend was valued for probate in 1404 at £3. (Charters and Records of Hereford Cathedral, p.262).

82   In 1420 parish chaplains in Hereford diocese received either 7 marks annually or 40 shillings with meals. In Monmouth they received the latter. (Regist. E. Lacy, p.87)

83   R. A. Griffiths, op. cit., p.157.

84   For the Monmouth tiles see H. G. Griffinhoofe, *The Mediaeval Tiles in St. Mary's Church*, 1894.

85   Transcribed by Canon A. T. Bannister in EHR, 1929, 1930.

86   Cal. Patent Rolls, 1391-1396, p.372.

87   Ibid., 1396-1399, pp.88, 111.

88   Ibid., 1399-1401, pp.179, 527.

89   R. R. Davies, op. cit., p.196.

Part Three
ROYALTY 1387 - 1485

1 Henry IV

John of Gaunt's young wife, Blanche, bore one son before she died, Henry Bolingbroke, Earl of Derby. In 1381 he married Mary de Bohun, joint heiress of the Earl of Hereford. She inherited in 1384 and three years later gave birth in Monmouth Castle to the future Henry V. In 1387 Derby, who had been made Duke of Hereford for his services to the crown, was banished to France, and two years later, when John of Gaunt died, Richard II revoked the letters patent permitting him to inherit the Duchy of Lancaster, and granted it instead to the Duke of Exeter.[1]

Henry was in Paris when he heard the news and in June 1399 he sailed from Boulogne for England. The king returned from Ireland to meet him but, finding himself deserted, surrendered to his cousin at Flint. When Richard abdicated, Henry claimed the throne as a descendant of Henry III and 'through the right which God had given him by conquest when the realm was nearly undone for want of governance'. His estates were merged with those of the crown and shortly afterwards his son Henry was declared Prince of Wales and Duke of Lancaster. Bolingbroke's success was mainly due to the organisation and strategic position of his Lancastrian estates. Monmouth Castle, for instance, was heavily guarded 'ad resistendum inimicos domini' from 1399 onwards.[2]

Henry IV was crowned on St. Edward's day and the sword Curtana, representing justice without vindictiveness, was carried by the young Prince of Wales. Amidst the panoply of the coronation, Adam of Usk watching in the sanctuary, noticed the series of misfortunes which befell the king: 'First, in the procession he lost one of his coronation shoes...secondly one of the golden spurs fell off...thirdly at the banquet a sudden gust of wind carried away the crown from his head'. Adam also noticed that he dropped his offering, and that after the anointing with oil, 'there ensued such a growth of lice especially on his head, that he neither grew hair, nor could he have his head uncovered for many months'.[3] The disasters these omens foretold were not long in appearing. In the year after his accession, trouble broke out in Wales which, in the person of Owain Glyn Dwr, was to disturb the whole reign, bring glory to Henry's son and destruction to the lordship of Monmouth.

Owain's achievement, it has been said, is not that he was the last Welshman to lead his country against England but that he was the first to unite it against anyone. It was the tragedy of that achievement that so much of the country suffered in the process. In Monmouth, the effects of the rebellion were more long-lasting than those that followed the plagues of the previous

Carving found in the River Wye near the bridge.

century and were more difficult to eradicate.

The town became aware of the threat in 1402, the year of the comet which terrified Europe but was seen as the blessing of God to Glyn Dwr. Two years earlier he had appeared in arms claiming the title of Prince of Wales which had already been conferred on Henry of Monmouth. Welshmen flocked to his standard and he was in Gwent by 1402. Monmouth appealed for help to the Duchy.[4] Reluctant officials in London offered to pay one-sixth of the cost of reinforcing the walls. Enough seems to have been done to keep the rebels out, but Owain's control of the surrounding countryside was sufficient to paralyse the life of the lordship and disrupt its economy for the next twenty years.

Owain, by this time, had acquired his reputation as a practitioner of the black arts, with complete control over the frightful Welsh weather. It was a reputation acknowledged by Shakespeare when he makes Owain tell Hotspur, 'I can call spirits from the vasty deep' and boast:

> Three times hath Henry Bolingbroke made head
> Against my power. Thrice from the banks of Wye
> And sandy bottomed Severn have I sent
> Him bootless home and weather beaten back.

In 1404, Henry of Monmouth, 17 years old, took command of the English army on the border. In that year the Welsh appeared in Archenfield and the forces of the two princes of Wales faced each other. The invasion of Archenfield was reported to the king by a panic-stricken Archdeacon of Hereford:

The Welsh rebels in great numbers have entered Archenfield and have burnt houses, killed the inhabitants, taken prisoners, ravaged the country to the insupportable damage of the county. We pray Our Sovereign Lord that he will come in his Royal Person, otherwise we shall be utterly destroyed, which God forbid. Written in haste at Hereford.[5]

The Welsh were defeated at Campston, near Abergavenny, by the Earl of Warwick but were reinvigorated by a successful skirmish at Craig y dorth near Trellech. The meagre information about this skirmish comes from a sixteenth century copy of the Annals of Glendower: 'In the same year was the slaughter of the Welsh at Campstone and another of the English at Craig y dorth...Here the more part of the English were slain and they were chased up to the Town Gate'.

The Welsh do not seem to have penetrated into Monmouth but their presence outside disrupted life to such an extent that courts could not be held, crops gathered, nor rents collected. It was the same at Skenfrith where the tenants were confined to the castle for safety while their pillaged lands decayed.[6] Similarly at Penallt, 'all the tenants left the Patria, and certain of them are killed, and their lands lie in the lord's hands for lack of tenants'.[7] All this made travel dangerous and expensive. The Duchy auditor had to spend 35s 2d on an escort to Brecon for 'security by road owing to thieves and other malefactors in those parts in time of insurrection by Owen de Glendourda'.[8]

The paralysis of manorial life and the difficulty of collecting rents meant that the Duchy officials were unable to present their accounts and as a result were in danger of being classed as rebels themselves. In 1404 no courts were held in the lordships of Monmouth, Grosmont, White Castle and Dingestow because, in the words of the accountants, 'the tenants are rebels'.[9] It was the same with many of the bond tenants captured by the Welsh in 1403; they were despoiled and often imprisoned, only to find on their release that they were rearrested for non-payment of rent while in rebel hands.[10]

For the lords themselves the difficulties were greater than after the Black Death because the remedies then available, the farming out of land to temporary lessees, could not apply to occupied territory. Occasionally land was recovered as when William Wexham was granted the lands of Robert Huntley, 'forfeited to the king on account of his rebellion and adherence to the Welsh rebels'[11] but there could be no assurance that such land would be cultivated. In fact, the Huntleys recovered their lands at Hadnock and by 1479 Hugh Huntley had become Justiciar of Wales.

Salvation came as a result of two battles, one at Grosmont where the Welsh were defeated by the combined forces of Gilbert Talbot, William Newport and Sir John Greyndor; the other at Usk where Lord Grey of Codnor defeated and captured Owain's eldest son Gruffydd. Salvation was one thing, the restoration of the lordship was more difficult. Owain remained a threat until 1410 when, on his last incursion into the Marches, he was defeated at Welshpool. Amongst those of his men taken prisoner was Philip Scudamore of Troy. He had been Master Sergeant of Monmouth, and in the early days of the revolt had been put in command of Carreg Cennen Castle where, when he found Owain's forces to be overwhelming, he defected. He was executed at Shrewsbury where Adam of Usk went to see his head over the Welsh bridge.[12]

Owain went back to Wales, the old king died, and in 1416 Henry V offered his enemy a pardon. By then he may have been dead; he was certainly no longer a threat. But the legends with which he was to be associated were already arising. Adam of Usk described his burial by night and how that secret burial place had become known to his enemies, 'so he was reburied. But where his body lies is unknown'. The mystery surrounding his burial gave rise to the belief that he was still alive and the reluctance of the bards to sing his elegy.

There were fewer doubts on the English side and it was at last possible to repair some of the ravages on the border. It was a slow process. As late as 1420 St. Maughans was lying 'wholly in decay'[13] and the mills at Troy, Dixton and Rockfield were derelict. Five years later, twenty years after Glyn Dwr had been anywhere near Monmouth, the town's accounts were £391 in arrear.[14] In an attempt to put this right, drastic action was taken against debtors and tenants. It had little effect as the preamble to the charter of 1447 made clear. But long before then the king, who according to Winston Churchill, was to be 'more deeply loved by his subjects of all classes than any king has been in England', had reigned and died.

2 Henry V

He was born, possibly in the Great Tower, possibly in the Gatehouse on 16 September 1387.[15] Numerous nineteenth century antiquaries have described his cradle, his nurses and his removal at an early age to Courtfield. His mother died when he was 7 years old. When his father was banished he was taken into the entourage of Richard II and was with the king in Ireland when his father returned.

He has been described by a contemporary: 'His head was round in shape, indicating wealth of judgement as well as wisdom, which is borne out further by the width of his forehead. He had a mass of smooth brown hair. His nose was straight and his face strikingly open. He had a florid complexion and an expression of great charm. His eyes were brown and shone as gently as a dove's when he was in a good humour, but flashed like a lion's when roused. He had snow white teeth, conspicuously regular. His ears were well shaped and small. He had a dimple on his chin...'[16]

The head of Henry V on the great screen in York Minster.

During his early life when commanding the royal forces against Glyn Dwr he had met many of the contemporaries who were to serve with him overseas. He was lucky in that they were all men of his own age, so that when they followed him to France they were at the peak of their fighting fitness. At Agincourt Henry was 28 and almost all his commanders were under 32. They had tasted victory with him in Wales and men like the Duke of York, the Earl of Warwick, Gilbert Talbot and Sir John Greyndor were ready to follow him where he led.

By then Glyn Dwr was little more than an outlaw, although as late as 1412 he had been able to capture and hold to ransom David Gam. Henry licensed the latter to collect the 200 marks needed by comortha (perambulation) in the surrounding lordships. Such a licence was necessary because of the measures introduced at the beginning of the rebellion, ostensibly against the bards, to prohibit 'wasters, rhymers, minstrels or vagabonds maintaining themselves by begging or comortha'. David Gam, 'a great stickler for the Duke of Lancaster', accompanied Henry to Agincourt with three men at arms and died on that battlefield. The organisation of that expedition, the marshalling of fifteen hundred vessels to carry the army, its horses and weapons to France, the discipline Henry maintained in appalling weather and his personal bravery and confidence in victory were the marks of a great commander.

There was, too, his religious faith. Until his death he contributed 1,000 marks a year towards the restoration of Westminster Abbey. Coupled with this was his belief that it was the duty of the king to oppose disruptive doctrines such as Lollardy. By the time the Battle of Agincourt began he was in all but name the head of the Church of England. And his men followed him. After he had given the order 'Banners advance in the name of Jesus, Mary and St. George', the whole army fell to its knees, made the sign of the cross and put a morsel of earth under the tongue in preparation for death. His religious fanaticism and insistence on absolute obedience led to his treatment of the Lollards, just as his determination to be the victor at Agincourt led to his killing of the prisoners. His attitude to death was typical of his age.

There is an enduring Monmouth tradition, shared by Powick in Worcestershire, that when Henry was returning from Calais he heard the French ringing their bells. He is said to have returned to the town, removed the offending bells, put them on a boat and then brought them to Monmouth (or Powick) and hung them in the tower of the parish church. This unlikely story seems to be based on the seventh Monmouth bell having one of the few remaining examples of Rudhall's black lettering in which *coelis* has been misread as Calais.

𝕳𝖆𝖇𝖊𝖔 𝖓𝖔𝖒𝖊𝖓 𝕮𝖆𝖇𝖗𝖎𝖊𝖑𝖎𝖘 𝖒𝖎𝖘𝖘𝖎 𝖉𝖊 𝖈𝖔𝖊 𝖑𝖎𝖘

In a reign that was short and orientated towards France he had little time to spare for Monmouth, yet in the year of his accession, he ordered a new gate and two towers to be built in Monmouth Castle 'in the best manner that ye know'. He stipulated that the cost should not exceed £100 but his fear of extravagance was groundless as only £29 was spent in the next three years. It was left to his son, Henry VI, to complete the work thirty years later.[17]

The Steward of Monmouth at this time was his old comrade-in-arms, Sir John Greyndor. Although tainted with Lollardy, the Greyndor family, through their services to John of Gaunt and careful marriages, had risen quickly to acquire many offices of state.[18] He was licensed to choose his own confessor,[19] and served with the king at Agincourt. He had a devout relative who left Hadnock to become an anchoress at Bristol. There she was paid 8d a week out of the petty customs of the port, to pray 'for the good estate of the king and for his soul after death and the souls of Mary his late consort and his father and mother'.[20]

The seal and signature of Henry V.

As Duke of Lancaster Henry appointed the prior in 1413[21] and in the same year ordered that arrears in a corrody granted by John of Gaunt to a certain William Benet should be paid immediately.[22] In 1415 he ordered his receiver to pay Sir John Greyndor the wages of twelve archers, six at White Castle and six in Monmouth.[23]

Henry also intervened in the borough over the old custom of exacting toll on the brewing of ale. Marcher lords had full control over weights, measures and tolls and in this case the 'castle coules' were the cause of discord. Henry IV had clarified the custom by ordering that any burgess who brewed ale for sale within the town should deliver to the castle 17 gallons for every brew, when the king, his heirs or his council were resident there. When none of them was at the castle, brewers were to pay 10d for every brew. This was confirmed by Henry V in 1417, with the added proviso that 'all our ministers for their dwelling in the castle there, shall have sufficient ale of the said "Castle cowles" for the time that they shall be occupied there in our service'.[24]

Thirty years later the charter of Henry VI granted the castle coules to the mayor, bailiffs and burgesses of Monmouth forever in return for a composite annual payment which covered many other tolls and privileges and was called the Fee Farm rent.

One of the last letters Henry wrote about Monmouth was also over a comparatively trivial administrative matter, the refusal of one of his auditors to pay a food and clothing allowance to the mayor and bailiffs. They regarded this payment of 1s every Monday and Saturday for their meals, and 46s 8d annually for their robes, as payment for collecting the rents, tolls and fines. The king ordered the auditor to continue the payments 'until our arrival in England from abroad, without molesting them or grieving them therefore in the meantime'.[25]

There is a transcription of this letter in the borough archives on which someone has written, 'The sentry on his post, looking in vain for that tomorrow he shall never see'. A little over a year later, 'Death drew his scythe across these prospects. The gleaming king, cut off untimely, went to his tomb amid the lamentations of his people, and the crown passed to his son, an infant nine months old'.

It was a bleak period in Monmouth's history, a time of insecurity and neglect. The assize roll of 1413 is indicative.[26] The assize was held before Walter Hungerford, Chief Steward of the Duchy lands south of the Trent, 'to hear and determine divers treasons, insurrections, and rebellions within the lordship of Monmouth'. It begins with a long list of tenants who did not appear before the justices on the first day of the sessions as they should have done. Each was fined 1s and the list includes the Prior of Monmouth, the Lord of Wyesham, the Vicar of Llangattock, the Chaplain John Ornell, the Clerk John Bryd, the Forester of Hadnock Chase (who was not fined) and fifty-seven others.

There follows a series of thefts, forestallings and trespasses; several affrays in the market with arms drawn; the receiving of a stolen falchion worth 8d; the theft from a Gloucestershire vicarage of books, towels, bedclothes and gold and silver spoons worth £10; the case of a man buying and selling in the market without paying toll; and an attempted murder with a 'gesarme' or pike.

Several men were prosecuted for offences committed ten years earlier in the rebellion, but as the assize coincided with the king's attempts to make peace with Glyn Dwr, most of them were pardoned. John Lybyk was accused of buying lead from the rebels who had, in turn, acquired it from White Castle. John Cook was accused of selling a horse for 7 marks to a rebel knowing that it would help him in his rebellion. Richard Stoote was accused of selling axes and leather bottles to the rebels, and Thomas Seriant was charged with granting a parson land at English Newton, knowing him to be a traitor.

Finally there was an item of 25s 4d from the borough to the king, 'for a recognition of the superior new lordship of Our Lord the King, and of his royalty over the burgesses and men of the same borough, recently obtained'.

It signified the acceptance by the new lord of all existing obligations and conditions, and an acknowledgement of the enhanced status conferred on the town by the fact that the Duke of Lancaster was also king.

While the assize was being held there was trouble with the receivers over the rent still owing since the rebellion. They had been ordered to bring the money to the king in London in 1409,[27] but when they failed to do so they had been replaced. A succession of new appointments followed, each new receiver being ordered to collect the arrears and then being reprimanded or arrested for failing to do so.[28] In 1425, when there was still £391 owing, the stewards of Monmouth and Kidwelly were told to make themselves responsible for selling all debtors' property, stop the leasing of all lands and mills by the reeves and take over the letting of the estate at the best possible value.[29]

Monmouth's own particular tribute to her king has been the ungainly statue on the Shire Hall. It was erected in 1792 by the common council, a few years after the four hundredth anniversary of his birth.[30] A more appropriate memorial is the King's Garden, at the back of the Castle and Regimental Museum with its s'graphiti by Otto Maciag showing Henry with his Queen after their marriage.

3 Henry VI

A child, nine months old, succeeded the great king. His uncle, John Duke of Bedford became Protector while, first Humphrey of Gloucester and then Cardinal Beaufort, presided over a contentious council. And as dissension increased the glory of the dead king's memory shone with increasing lustre.

Three years after his death a message reached Monmouth about certain of the royal jewels which had been pledged to Thomas ap Henry by the king when raising money for the French War. Thomas had advanced the money in return for the jewels but had then been killed at Agincourt. The jewels were collected by the auditor, and the receiver was ordered to return them to London with all possible speed.[31]

During Henry VI's reign Monmouth had a brief return to literary fame when George Ashby became Master Sergeant in 1438. Rather like Henry of Grosmont, though on a minor scale, he combined his official duties with writing. He was a didactic poet of some renown.[32] He left Monmouth for the court and by 1450 was Clerk of the Signet to Henry VI and later to Margaret of Anjou. As a Lancastrian, he was in the Fleet prison by 1463 where he began writing a long poem, *A Prisoner's Reflections*:

> George Ashbys ys my name that ys greved
> By enprysonment a hoole yere or more...

He seems to have become responsible for the education of the young Prince Edward until his murder in 1471. In this role he produced two long poems, the Latin translated into English verse; *The Active Policy of a Prince* and *Dicta Philosophorum*. It is not great poetry but the advice is sound, and if Edward could have kept to one half of it he would have made a wise king:

> A kynge shude be right busy and studious
> To goveurne his Reaulme and his people pur,
> As a Gardyner is right laborous
> To kepe hys gardeyne clene from wedys seure...

Or again, advice that was as applicable in the fifteenth century as it is today:

> Every man hath one Mouth and two eres,
> To thentente that he sholde here more than speke...
> So, in litil speche and right muche heryng,
> Many grete vertues is conquering.

The reign was also remarkable because of the belief in the king's ability to work miracles. Those in need of a cure were measured in string which was then doubled and coated with wax to make a candle which was taken to the church by a member of the family. The same method had been used when seeking the help of St. Thomas of Hereford in the early fourteenth century.

The aftermath of the Welsh rebellion continued to trouble the lordship for another twenty years. In 1406 the effect was immediate. Monmouth, Dixton, Llanrothal, Whitchurch and Llangarron, amongst others, were excused payment of the King's Aid owing to the devastation caused by the rebellion. Twenty years later, Whitchurch and Llanrothal were exempt because they had fewer than ten parishioners. Monmouth Priory was exempt in 1426, 1432, 1445 and at regular intervals until 1492.[33]

Fugitive bondsmen were still being arrested in 1447 and for many years there were accusations of treachery. The most important of these concerned John Scudamore who had married Alice, one of Glyn Dwr's daughters, and had become constable of Monmouth in 1425. Information was laid against him by Edmund Beaufort on the legal grounds that no Englishman married to a Welsh woman should remain in office. This had been one of the restrictive measures introduced by Henry IV in 1402. Beaufort was not disinterested in this and, when Scudamore was dismissed, he was appointed steward and constable in his place.[34]

The long term effects of the rebellion on the priory were mainly financial, but a decline in the quality of religious life continued. William Eyton, who had been appointed prior by Henry V in 1413, was authorised to receive ecclesiastics into the priory and subject them to the rule of St. Benedict in order to improve the tone of divine service, *'cultum divinii servicii ampliandum'*.[35] Twenty years later, the bishop hearing that the prior was 'slowly paying the debt of all flesh', ordered the priory to be sequestrated by the Duchy, giving as his reason 'the many and great inconveniences [which] happened to the priory through the stupid carelessness of those resident there, which threatened to overthrow the same, just as they now threaten it with manifest [ruin] if no help or remedy be found for unusual expenditure'.[36]

Among the more usual items of expenditure were corrodies and pensions. The priory had little control over the former which were annuities usually imposed by outsiders for the benefit of outsiders, but pensions were an internal affair and of benefit to the monks themselves. Priors were particularly favoured, provided the assent of the bishop and the incoming prior had been obtained. Thus in 1445 Richard Horton retired with a pension of 10 marks.[37] Two years later his successor retired with a pension of £5, or £4 with food, drink and rooms in the priory.[38] The amount rose steadily until, in 1524, Richard Burton received £14 6s 0d annually with food, drink and a private room.[39]

By then the diocese had been set an example in these matters by Thomas Wolsey who became Dean of Hereford in 1512. A few months later he resigned, never having resided at the cathedral, with an annual pension for three years, followed by £40 a year for life. His letter of resignation is indicative of the general attitude to such perquisites. After a fawning introduction, he asks 'for just reasons to be relieved of the burden, care and rule of the Deanery'. He then expresses the hope that 'a pension may be assigned...from the revenues of the said Deanery' and ends majestically, 'otherwise I do not resign'.[40]

Throughout the fifteenth century criminals arraigned before the ecclesiastical courts appeared in Monmouth to do penance or secure purgation. A typical instance of the former was the punishment by the Bishop of Hereford of Thomas ap Roger who had been present when a priest was murdered in 1432. He was sentenced to visit St. Mary's church in Monmouth, 'naked to the waist, barefoot, and with a halter round his neck, with arms bound and carrying a rod in his hands'. He was to be flogged by priests while 'reciting a penitential psalm before the door of the church when the greater number of people should be present, openly confessing his crime'.

This was to be repeated at Skenfrith, Kentchurch and Grosmont and, finally, before the Bishop in Hereford Cathedral on Easter Day. He was to make restitution to the church in which the murdered man had served and, either fast every weekday in Lent, or abstain from milk food for the rest of his life. When absolution was finally granted, he recited his offence to the bishop 'in mournful tones'.[41] His accomplices, the actual murderers, received no punishment at all, both receiving absolution without performing penance; Roger ap Jenan Bythan because he was not strong enough and David ap John because he had 'gone into remote parts, not daring to perform penance because of animosities in the neighbourhood'.

Clerics, when summoned before secular courts, were remanded into the custody of the Bishop of Hereford, being escorted there by a local vicar. Thus, John Barre, vicar of Dixton, was commissioned to perform that duty in 1431[42] and John Marees, vicar of Monmouth, in 1492.[43] Once in the bishop's care they were usually released after purgation, and the ease with which purgation was obtained may partly explain the frequency of clerical crime. All that happened to Rees Kynwyn, a clerk convicted of theft, was an announcement in Monmouth market that the bishop had accepted his purgation and granted his immediate release.[44] It was little more than a formality and may be the reason why the prior of Monmouth, who was in prison in 1479, remained in office for another three years.[45]

The David ap John who was unable to perform penance because of animosity in the neighbourhood had a namesake one hundred years later who was a Monmouth priest and a native of Dixton. He was cited in St. Mary's, by order of the bishop, on the grounds that he had been found guilty of incontinence with Alice Philpotts, and had remained obdurate, though frequently told to put her away. The clergy of Archenfield were ordered to alert their flocks to the danger from this wolf in clerical clothing, and to warn them against hearing any mass said by David, 'nay, to absent themselves...that he may the more speedily be moved to penitence and the fruits of better living'.[46] Although these warnings may have separated him from his flock, they did not separate him from Alice, and in 1530 the bishop was reduced to writing to Henry VIII imploring him to arrest David for 'repeated contumacy, he being excommunicated and remaining obdurate'.[47]

Another priest called William Glover, 'alias Glovare' late of Monmouth, was at that time in the bishop's gaol at Hereford for breaking into a house in Monmouth and stealing a pair of stockings and a white woollen cloth worth 4s. He was released after giving surety for good behaviour.[48]

When, at the outbreak of the Hundred Years War, the alien priories were severed from their parent abbeys in France, the annual payments, 10 marks in the case of Monmouth, were diverted to the crown. By 1442, when the war was coming to a close, Monmouth's money was being paid to William Byngham, the rector of St. John Zachary in London.[49] He was the founder of God's House, Cambridge, the predecessor of Christ's College, and from 1458 onwards the money was paid to the college at his request.[50]

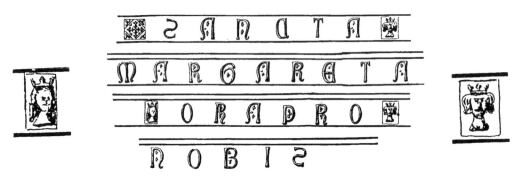

Lettering on the great bell at Dixton with the heads of Edward III and his queen as stops. The only Royal Head Bell in the county, c1420.

A rental of the priory in mid-century shows the monks holding twenty-five burgages, 'the Wynyerd', demesne land at Hadnock, the tithe of Hadnock weir, Mallybrook mill, two parcels of land in St. Thomas's churchyard, several crofts and tenements and 2 acres of land which were let to the Hospital of St. Michael.[51] This hospital lay at Chapel Farm, now demolished and buried under the embankment of the A40. It was near Hadnock weir and a mediaeval crossing of the Wye on the Royal Way from Staunton to Monmouth. It had been founded for the relief of the poor and infirm. Indulgences for those assisting it with alms were granted in 1427, 1464 and 1522. Nothing now remains of the chapel except the font in Dixton Church. Nor are there any remains of the Chapel of St. Nicholas at Dixton which received a bequest from Hugh Huntley in 1501.[52]

Local legends associated Chapel Farm with a leper hospital, and these in turn have taken substance from a hospital 'outside the East gate' which was founded by John of Monmouth in the thirteenth century. Leprosy ceased to be a serious threat in the fifteenth century, and it is possible that an older hospital near the ford was rededicated to St. Michael when its purpose was changed. But there is nothing in the documents to suggest a leper hospital, just as it is most unlikely that the legendary 'leper seat' on the south wall of the chancel at Dixton was ever allowed to accommodate lepers.

Other indulgences were granted to those helping David the Hermit to repair the chapel of St. Mary Magdalene at Dixton in 1515[53] and to those helping with the repair of the chapel of St. Thomas the Martyr at Wyesham in 1479.[54] They were also granted to the innumerable collectors for charity permbulating the diocese at this time. These collectors were often proctors of hospitals, but could include such diverse characters as Brother Clement, a monk from Mount Sinai,[55] and Thomas ap Jonys, 'lately mayor on Monmouth', who was licensed to go round the diocese begging in 1509 after he had been reduced to poverty when his house caught fire.[56]

The church of St. Mary had been enriched during the fifteenth century by a collection of tiles used both murally and on the floor. Many of these which were of Malvern type were made locally at the tile kiln recently uncovered in Monk Street.[57] Ridge roof tiles and bricks were also made there. The surviving tiles from the mediaeval church were removed when the church was rebuilt in the eighteenth century and set in the baptistry walls. They were removed and cleaned recently and are now in the south aisle. Two with a Monmouth connection are the tiles bearing the white swan enchained of Henry V's mother, Mary de Bohun and a fine large heraldic one made for Thomas and Alice Coke.[58]

Tile in St. Mary's Church showing the white swan enchained.

Tile of Thomas and Alice Coke in St. Mary's Church.

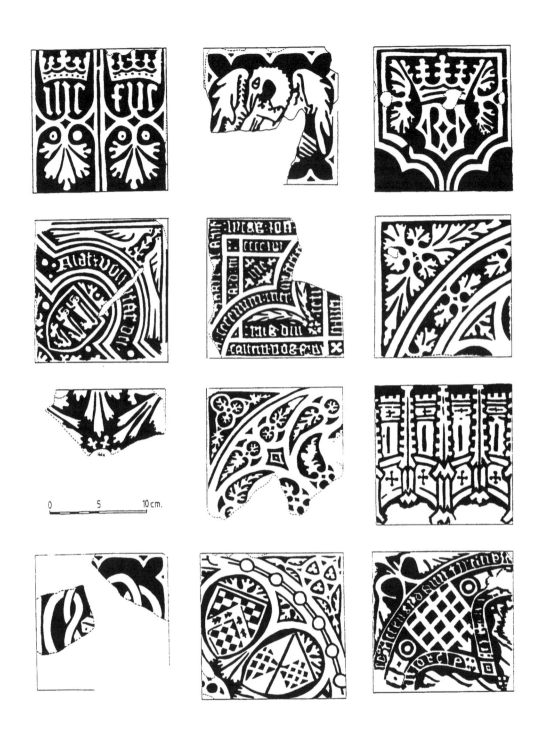

A selection of tiles of the Malvern School, made in the kiln recently discovered by the Monmouth Archeological Society at Cadogan House, Monk Street, Monmouth. This is one of only two kilns of the Malvern School discovered outside Great Malvern.

4 The Borough

In 1447 Monmouth received its earliest known charter of incorporation. There were possibly earlier ones but this is the first to have survived in its entirety. Contemporary with it is a group of documents which throw some light on the character of the town, and the life and problems of its inhabitants. Certainly the town had begun to take the shape that has survived today. Monnow Street (once the Great Causey), Whitecross Street (a white cross usually denoted a plague cross), Wyebridge Street, Drybridge, Cinderhill Street, St. Mary Street, Butchers Row (Church Street), Greindor Street (Glendower Street), Monk Street, Weirhead Street and the central market place provided a skeleton which has changed little in 500 years. Until the coming of the A40 and peripheral council estates, the only major operation on this skeleton was the incision of Priory Street through the Bull Ring in the early nineteenth century.

A few streets have disappeared or been renamed, but none can have been important. Smythes Street and Gryme Street may have been the same, possibly Nailers' Lane. Whychestrete led to the Whyche or Wicket Gate of the castle; Peterslane led from Dixton gate to Dixton church; and Inch Lane, a common name for any narrow passage, has been used for Bell Lane, Worcester Street and the Back Lane off Agincourt Street.

In 1441 the king had asked John Ireland, the Mayor of Great Monmouth, to furnish him with a list of burgesses, resident and non-resident, in both Great and Little Monmouth, and for the names of 'any men who, by fraud

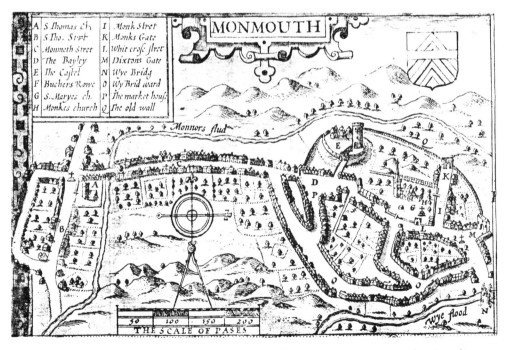

Great and Little Monmouth (Overmonnow) joined by Monnow Street on John Speed's map in 1610.

and collusion, have in any ways purchased any burgages or parcels of burgages there, and who by means of such purchases...may be quit and discharged from toll and custom'.[59] He was also instructed to assist the collector of 'our old custom there called chence money'. This was an annual payment of 1s by landless Welshmen called chencers, giving them the right to trade in the town on certain days.

The mayor began his answer to the king's letter with the assurance that there were no fraudulent burgesses in the town, that there were seventy-nine resident and two non-resident burgesses in the borough of Monmouth, and ninety-one resident in Little Monmouth 'who claim liberty within the borough'. There were also twenty-nine who had been appointed by the prior and who claimed similar borough liberty.[60] The latter were still unpopular and the mayor complained that 'the prior and convent claim to make burgesses in their courts henceforth and for time to come'. Such courts, held before the prior's steward, involved the declaration of fealty to the prior by the new burgess and the payment of the customary shilling if he was the son of a burgess and half a mark if he was not.[61]

The total of 201 burgesses compares favourably with the 266 mentioned in a Duchy survey of the town in 1610, and on a conservative estimate would give a population of about 1,000. But it was not considered enough for prosperity and in 1447, Henry VI tried to remedy this by charter. Although there was a well-established civic administration, Monmouth was a borough by prescription, and Henry's charter was one of incorporation. It became the model for succeeding charters and for that reason is dealt with in some detail.

It opens with a preamble which shows how heavily the shadow of Glyn Dwr still hung over the town, and how readily everyone attributed their ills to his brief incursion into the outskirts some forty years earlier:

Know ye that We, mindful how that the burgesses of Our Town and Borough of Monmouth in the March of Wales within our Duchy of Lancaster, have suffered manifold and no small losses and burnings of their houses, and divers oppressions which the Welshmen, out of their malice, heretofore often inflicted on them, and hence the said Town, which is an ancient borough of the Duchy aforesaid, is now, as it were for the greater part waste and derelict for want of burgesses dwelling there.[62]

The charter goes on to promise certain privileges which will 'provide more abundantly, as well for the aid and relief of the said Town and Borough of Monmouth, as for the welfare, peace and quiet of the burgesses'. They are summarised here in the order in which they occur.

1   That the burgesses shall have a commonalty from which they may choose annually, on the day after the feast of St. Michael, one mayor and two bailiffs from amongst themselves. They are to take their oaths before the receiver or auditor in the Exchequer of Monmouth.
2   That the mayor may choose two ministers who may carry each of them 'one mace with Our arms of Our Duchy engraven on them'. (The

mayor himself carried a white stick and the bailiffs staves. By 1566 they were carrying glaives.)

3   That the mayor, officers and burgesses shall be a corporate body, capable of buying and owning land in the name of the mayor, bailiffs and commonalty of the town and borough of Monmouth. (They were slow in acquiring land, and by 1580 held only 3.5 acres of Pyrle's Orchard on Chippenham).

4   That they may plead and be impleaded in the same name.

5   That the commonalty shall have the town and borough of Monmouth, with the markets, fairs, stallages, piccages, dues, chenses and all other profits, customs and tolls, including the rent of assize of the burgages and the 'castle coules'.

6   That the burgesses may have the Hundred (court) of Monmouth, and all profits, fines and amercements arising therefrom.

7   That the mayor and bailiffs shall hold pleas by writ of right, and exercise jurisdiction over all pleas and cases arising within the bounds of the borough and foreignry.

8   That the bounds of the borough be 'the bridge of Malibrooke, Brodstone, Redbroke, the bridge of Liteltroye, Portefelde, Cadeputte [Bailey Pit], Ricardesforde and Maynston Crosse [Manson's Cross]'.

9   That the mayor and bailiffs shall be Justices of the Peace within the borough and foreignry, with power to impose fines on felons and exercise all the duties of justices.

10   That the burgesses shall be empowered to elect one Coroner from amongst themselves every year.

11   That no burgess, nor tenant of a burgess, nor his heirs shall be compelled to answer for a crime before any Duchy Court except the Justices in Eyre or the Chief Steward of the Duchy. 'Nor shall any of them be convicted or tried within the lordships [of Monmouth and the Three Castles] by any foreigners, but by Englishmen of the said Borough, and not by any Welshmen for ever'.

12   That no fairs or markets shall be held within five miles of the said borough, and that the market there shall be held 'within the walls of the said borough in the place usual and accustomed, on Wednesday and Saturday every week, and not elsewhere as has been customary'.

13   That the mayor and bailiffs shall have power to punish forestalling and regrating by fines which shall be levied for the use of the burgesses.

14   That the mayor and bailiffs shall have the Assize of Bread, Wine and Ale, as well as Weights, Measures and Scales, without any interference from Duchy officials.

15   That all burgesses shall be allowed to bequeath burgages and chattels, and shall not be liable for any common gifts, tallages or aids, except those appertaining to the borough.

16   That no burgess, his heir, tenant or servant, shall be liable for the debts of his neighbours, unless he be the principal debtor or pledge, and

in the latter case he shall not be distrained for the debt so long as the principal debtor can pay.

17 'Rendering yearly unto Us and Our heirs by the hand of Our Receiver of Monmouth for the time being, Twenty and seven pounds at the feasts of Easter and Saint Michael Archangel, in equal portions, for all services, customs and demands'.

18 That the power of the Chief Steward, Receiver and Auditor shall be in no way affected or diminished.

19 That the powers of the Justices in Eyre shall, similarly be in no way affected by the charter.

20 'Given at Our palace of Westminster on the 17th day of July in the 25th year, etc. of Henry VI. By bill sealed under Signet of the Eagle, signed with the sign manual of the king himself, and of the date aforesaid by authority of Parliament'.

Some of these rights went back to 1256 (no. 16), others had been acquired by custom. Some arose out of the Welsh rebellion (no. 11), although as early as the reign of Edward I an ordinance had stated that no Welshman was to reside in a walled borough. It was largely ignored and by 1400 Welshmen formed a substantial proportion of the population of Monmouth. Some of the rights (no. 10) were new. The Fee Farm Rent of £27 (no. 17) continued to be paid with ever diminishing enthusiasm to the lord of the manor until 1927 when the Borough Council bought itself out for £531 5s 0d. For comparison the Fee Farm of Hereford in 1189 was £40.

The borough boundaries have changed very little and are still recognisable. So too are the parish boundaries, which were recorded in detail in 1432 when Richard le Messager, 'a native of Monmouth, a layman, 40 years of age and of free condition', gave evidence before a court in Hereford.[63] His account of each specific bound is so clear that his instructions can be followed by anyone walking them today. He was helping to define the boundaries with Llandaff which was a question troubling the Bishop of Hereford, Thomas Spofford. The diocese had been without a bishop for six years and he came from being Abbot of St. Mary's, York to cope with 'a wild diocese, needing a strong man to rule it'.

Just as the boundaries were known, so were the field names, and these with the streets and bridges, provide a topographical picture of Monmouth which conforms in most ways to the town that existed up to the First World War. Less is known about the people who inhabited it, but the Coroner's Roll for the years 1449 to 1452 reveals something of their follies and crimes.

Coroners were first appointed in 1194 but it was not until 1447 that Monmouth refers to such an official. His principal duty was to hold inquests on the bodies of the dead. On receiving information from 'the first finder' he was expected to go immediately to inspect the body.[64] Then, with the help of between twelve and twenty-four jurymen, he had to decide the cause of death, arrest any suspects, appraise the dead man's possessions, and deliver a sealed report. The Monmouth roll, one of very few from mid-fifteenth century, records eight deaths, four from misfortune and four from violence.[65]

John Matthew and Henry Coly went out in a boat to mend the weir below Wye Bridge. This was a weir which, with the fishing, was to be leased for twelve years to Richard Vaughan and three others in 1460. On this occasion the boat was overloaded with stones and sand. Both Matthew and Coly were drowned. The jury found that the stones, the weir, the water and the boat were the causes of their deaths and that, therefore, they should be forfeited into the king's hands. This was a deodand, literally a gift to God in which the instruments of death were forfeited to the lord so that they could be applied to pious uses, either directly or from the proceeds of the sale. Deodands continued to be exacted until the middle of the nineteenth century. The *Monmouthshire Merlin* for 1835 records one of £1 on a bull which gored a man to death and another of 2s on the wheel of a wagon which killed a boy near Ross.[66]

Misfortune or folly put an end to Henry Grenelefe, a tanner 'burnt with fire', when he set a lighted candle on his bed. As the candle was the cause of death and was consumed with the victim there was no deodand. There was nothing to forfeit either when Henry Wright, on his way home to Osbaston, fell into the Monnow and was drowned.

Violence accounted for the other four. John Andrews was slain by a Welshman called John ap Howel Gwyn 'in a certain mill called Monewmyll'. The murder was committed with a dagger worth 6d. A second death occurred further up the Monnow at Brookeshomme where John Cuffe was stabbed by a Welshman called John ap Phelpot ap Nichol. The third English victim was Edmund Taillour who was beaten to death in a field called Selnorsmede by Meurice ap Howel ap Thomas ap Sicel. The last was an all-English affray in Monkestrete where David Elvell slew John Smyth with a saw. In the last three cases the goods and chattels of the murderers were forfeited to the king.

The names of the jurors sitting with the coroner are predominantly occupational in origin and reveal something of the trades practised in the town at this time: Rees Baker, Richard Hosier, Richard Fflechier, Nicholas Corviser, John Carpenter, William Skorier, John Taillour, Edward Drover, Thomas Sadeler, Thomas Bochor, Hugh Dier, John Mason, Thomas Tanner, John Walle, to name but a few. There were also the Welshmen and, although the Duchy was a strongly Anglicising influence, they predominated outside the town. Thus, in 1397 it was alleged that the chaplain at Garway was 'unfitted to the cure of souls because he is ignorant of the Welsh language, and because the majority of the parishioners at this place do not know the English language'. Thirty years later the parish of Llangarron was not fully taxed because part of it was considered to be in Wales, *'quia quarta pars parochia non est infra comitatum Herefordie sed infra Wallia'*.[67]

There is little evidence about the guilds in Monmouth until 1427 when there was trouble over the authority by which four men were exercising the mystery of tanning and cordwainery. The king ordered that two honest towns-men should periodically inspect their work. He raised their amercement but allowed them to continue to ply their trade. Councillors were always jealous of the guilds and in 1706 they were annoyed by the formation of a fraternity of barbers, joiners, coopers, glaziers and flax dressers.[68]

In 1445 Henry VI had given orders that the gatehouse of the castle 'in which Our dearest father of famous memory was born', should be repaired and rebuilt as far as was necessary.[69] A certain Thomas Ornell, who later became mayor, was appointed to supervise the work. Over the next six years he spent about £60 on 'the new tower at the entrance of the castle'.[70] At about the same time, the great tower known as the 'dongeon', was repaired, along with the chapel and the king's two great chambers.[71] The building was to be partially paid for by the fines of felons and the goods of fugitive bondsmen. Henry Coley was to collect the money and the goods in 1445 but two years later he was discharged 'for certain immense and enormous transgressions and offences whereof he was accused by the Council'.[72]

In 1461 Edward, Duke of York, won the battle of Mortimer's Cross near Leominster and shortly afterwards was proclaimed king. He had been greatly helped by Sir William Herbert of Raglan who was rewarded firstly by being made Steward of Monmouth, and then being granted the Marcher Lordship of Raglan.[73] This was a new creation and included the manor of Dingestow which had been part of the lordship of Monmouth for centuries.

By letters patent in 1471, Edward IV granted to the bur-gesses of Monmouth almost the same privileges as those granted by Henry VI. During this reign the Chancery of Monmouth ac-quired a new seal.[74] It shows Edward, as Duke of Lancaster, in armour and has the words: S: EDWARDI: DI: GRA: REG: ANGL: T: FRANCIE: CANCELLARIE: SUE: DE: MONEMOUTH.

Seal of the chancery of Monmouth.

The Wars of the Roses had little effect on life in Monmouth, though the constant changes in the stewardship reflect the violence and uncertainty of the times. But in 1485 Henry Tudor landed at Milford Haven from exile in Brittany. Marching under the Red Dragon of Cadwaladr, he met Richard at Bosworth Field on 22 August and when evening came the kingdom was in the hands of the first of the Tudors while the naked body of the last Plantagenet was ex-hibited to the country folk tied to the back of a horse. It could be argued that the prophecies of Geoffrey of Monmouth had been fulfilled.

Henry was not the first monarch to realise that Geoffrey could be useful, but he was astute enough to use the prophecies as a means of bolstering his claim to the throne. He adopted a coat of arms quartering England, France, Brutus, Belinus, Arthur, Swain, Edward the Confessor and William the Conqueror; and when his first son was born he was christened Arthur. Many years later, Francis Bacon wrote that the prince was named Arthur 'in honour of the British race of which himself [Henry VII] was...according to that ancient worthy, King of the Britaines, in whose acts there is truth enough to make him famous, besides that which is fabulous'. Enthusiasm for the British History was encouraged by Caxton's publication of the *Chronicles of England*, and the Arthurian legends became a renewed source of national pride. As Edward Hall wrote in 1542 when describing the christening of Prince Arthur, 'Englishmen no more rejoysed than outward nations and foreign princes trembled and quaked, so much was that name to all nations terrible and formidable'.

A few months after Bosworth, Henry VII rewarded one of those who had fought at his side, Hugh ap Howell. In a letter to the mayor and bailiffs of Monmouth he ordered them to pay part of the Fee Farm Rent, 'in consideration of the faithful service which Our well beloved subject, Hugh ap Howell, did unto Us at Our victorious field, where it happened to him to be sore hurt and maimed. We, of Our grace especial, have given unto him by way of reward the sum of £20, and have appointed him to be paid the same by your hands, of Our fee farm of Our said Town'.[75]

One of the results of the new financial arrangements which the charter of 1447 introduced into local affairs was that the minister's accounts no longer show such items as rents of assize, chence money, tolls of the pyx or the castle coules, all of which were now collected by the mayor to pay for the fee farm.

The details of the manor, however, show some Welsh dues still being paid in 1491/2; Kilth, for instance, which produced 30s.[76] Many of the rents, formerly payable in kind, had been commuted to money payments: 6s the price of six sparrow hawks; 5s the price of 4 lbs of pepper (the rent of the manor of Wyesham); 1s 8d the price of 5 lbs of cummin; 8d the price of two geese (the rent of two tenements). Similarly at Hadnock, the customary works had been commuted to money: '849 customary works...sold by the corn reeve for 1d each work' and '807 customary works at reaping the lord's corn sold for $\frac{1}{2}$d each'. The church scot, an annual payment by Martinmas, was fixed at 6s 4d, the price of seventy-five hens.

These same accounts show rents increased for tenants who were procuring small parcels of land, about 3 feet wide, against their houses, to build chimneys on. These, replacing the open hearth in the middle of the floor, were built against the outer wall of the house before the wall was pierced to open up a fireplace. There was opposition from the die-hards who maintained that the smoke from the old open hearth, not only hardened the timbers but prevented disease. Nearly a hundred years later (1587) William Harrison still condemned them: 'Now we have many chimnies, and yet our tenderlings complain of many rheums, catarrhs and poses. Then we had none but reredoses and our heads did never ache'.

Although there was talk of the building of a court house, the accounts of 1492 do not give a very favourable economic picture. The farm of the fishery of the Wye brought in only 5s and the fishery of the Monnow had been 'thrown down' by order of the council. The New Mill, 'destroyed and laid waste in the time of the rebellion', had not been rebuilt one hundred years later. The 29 acres of Kyngesmede produced only half of what was customary 'because the greater part of the said meadow and pasture is overgrown with thorns and briers'. Thorns and briers filled the castle ditch and ivy covered the towers and walls. The lamp was still burning before the altar of the Holy Cross but the castle chapel had become a chantry of Grace Dieu. No honey or wax was collected and nothing came from the wood of Coedbuchan, where 'slatters' were quarried because there was no lessee. The stallage in the market and at the Barton produced nothing for the same reason. Even the fairs had been lost and, when the mayor and burgesses appealed to the king for a July fair, they explained that there were no fairs in the neighbourhood and that, if the Duchy granted one, it would be a great relief to the inhabitants.[77] This request was to be granted in the reign of Edward VI. So the town was not in the best condition to resist changes which were to alter its status as a Marcher lordship with a Benedictine Priory in the next century.

REFERENCES Part Three

(Abbreviations for some of the more frequently cited sources appear on page 8)

[1] Cal. Fine Rolls, 1391-1399, pp.293, 297.
[2] DL 29/615/9840.
[3] Chronicon (Edn. 1904) p 298.
[4] P.R.O. DL 42/15, f. 120.
[5] Quoted by A. T. Bannister, *The History of Ewyas Harold.*
[6] D. C. Somerville, *The Duchy of Lancaster*, I, pp.168-170.
[7] P.R.O. Ministers' Accounts 928/19 m.5.
[8] Ibid., 615/9841.
[9] Ibid., 729/12003/5. Henry IV.
[10] DL 42/16 fd. 158 v.
[11] Cal. Patent Rolls. 5 Henry IV, pt. I, p.238.
[12] Adam of Usk, *Chronicon*, p.296.
[13] P.R.O. Ministers' Accounts, 594/9514 8 Henry V.
[14] Somerville, op. cit., pp.216/7 (DL 42/18 fos. 264 v, 269).
[15] The Shire Hall statue states that he was born on August 9th. September 16th is now preferred.
[16] Memorials of Henry V, (1858), pp.64, 65.
[17] History of the King's Works, H.M.S.O., II, p.739.
[18] R. A. Griffiths, op. cit., pp.235-237.
[19] Regist. R. Mascall, p. 23.
[20] Cal. Patent Rolls, Henry IV, 1401/4, p.34.
[21] Regist. R. Mascall, p. 179.
[22] P.R.O. Misc. Bks. 17, fo. 25d.
[23] DL Misc. Bks. 3 Henry V.
[24] P.R.O. Misc. Bks. fos. 6 and 32.

25   P.R.O. DL 42/17, f. 166.

26   MBA. Transcription of Assize Roll, no. 1152, fo. 16/19. 1 Henry V.

27   P.R.O. DL 42/16, f. 28.

28   See R. A. Griffiths, op. cit., pp.183/185.

29   P.R.O. DL 42/18, fo. 264 x, 269.

30   A deplorable statue made by Charles Peart of Welsh Newton. He exhibited at the Royal Academy and modelled for Wedgwood. The s'graffiti by Otto Maciag was completed in 1993.

31   MBA. Transcription of DL Misc. Bks. Warrant Bk. fo. 35d.

32   Early English Text Society: *George Ashby's Poems.* Ed. Bateson, 1899.

33   P.R.O. Feudal Aids.

34   P.R.O. DL 42/18 fo. 10. For Scudamore see R. A. Griffiths, op. cit., pp.139-141.

35   Regist. R. Mascall, p.85.

36   Regist. T. Spofford, p.139.

37   Regist. J. Stanbury, p.16.

38   Regist. J. Stanbury, p.44.

39   Regist. C. Booth, p.148, 338.

40   Regist. R. Mayhew, p.148.

41   Regist. T. Spofford, p.157.

42   Ibid., p.132.

43   Regist. T. Mylling, p.147.

44   Ibid., p.132.

45   Ibid., p.54.

46   Regist. C. Booth, p.190.

47   Ibid., p.244.

48   Ibid., p.231.

49   Cal. Patent Rolls 10/6/1442.

50   Ibid., 25/6/1458.

51   MBA. Transcript of P.R.O. Rentals and Surveys: Roll 643.

52   Regist. J. Stanley, p.49. Hugh Huntley of Hadnock, Deputy Justice of South Wales, asked in his will to be buried in the chapel of St. Nicholas. (Cant. Cathedral Regist., fo. 26, quoted by R. A. Griffiths, op. cit., pp.156-158).

53   Regist. R. Mayhew, p.287.

54   Regist. T. Mylling, p. 206.

55   Regist. C. Booth, p. 356.

56   Regist. R. Mayhew, p. 288.

57   S. Clarke, *Medieval Ceramics*, vol. 16, 1992, pp 72-76.

58   The best local example of the swan enchained, Mary de Bohun's crest, a large lead figure, was recently stolen from the Swan Yard.

59   P.R.O. DL 37/9 No. 64.

60   The *Monmouthshire Gazette* published the mayor's reply in February, 1852, but the original has been lost.

61   MBA. Transcript of the Proceedings in the Prior's Court, 30 and 24 Henry VI.

62   The charters are kept in the Monmouth Museum.

63   Regist. T. Spofford, p.144.

64   R. F. Hunnisett, *The Mediaeval Coroner*, C.U.P., 1961.

65   P.R.O. DL Misc. Bks. 11/5 Monmouth.

66   *Monmouthshire Merlin* 23/5/1835 and 30/5/1835.

67   Visitation of Bishop Trefnant, 1397 and P.R.O. Feudal Aids, (1428-1431) II, p.404.

68   MBA. Council Minutes: 29/11/1706.

69   P.R.O. DL 37/12 m 6 d.

70   P.R.O. DL 29/616/9870.

71   P.R.O. DL 29/616/9872, 9875

72   MBA: Transcript from Great Cowcher, fo. 105, 115.

73 Cal. Patent Rolls, 1461-1467. 9/3/1465.

74 Now in National Museum of Wales. It was embedded in the wall of a cottage in the Forest of Dean in the nineteenth century. The owner said he found it in the Wye and used it as a weight for the pendulum of his clock.

75 MBA: Transcript with Ref. P.R.O. Letters 1 Henry VII.

76 MBA: Transcript of Ministers' Accounts, 1491/2.

77 Somerville, op. cit., p.313 (DL 12/1/6).

Part Four
REFORMATION AND RENEWAL 1530-1675

1 The Priory

Between Henry VIII's break with Rome and the Elizabethan Act of Settlement fifty years later, a deliberate attempt was made to dismember a system which had given faith and comfort to most English people for many centuries. The liturgy, with its seventy days of fasting and its recurring saints' days, had brought order and self-discipline to the country. On the other hand, the many saints' days reduced the number of working days, and this was especially harmful at harvest time.

One of the first reforms introduced in 1536 was the Act for the Abrogation of Holy Days. Amongst the saints' days removed in July alone were those of St. Martin, St. Swithun, St. Anne, St. Margaret, St. Mary Magdalene (restored in 1541) and the Translation of Becket's relics. This caused confusion as it destroyed the liturgical calendar at a time when there was no regular secular one. A saint who would not have been popular after the break with Rome was included in the date of the proceedings of the Hundred Court at Monmouth in 1449.

Heading of the proceedings of the Hundred Court in 1449

The state of the priory when the sixteenth century dawned is not easy to establish. There had been considerable enrichment of the buildings with the placing of the fine oriel over the entrance in the last years of the previous century. St. Mary's Church had been given new status by William Herbert of Troy, who asked in his will in 1524 to be buried 'on the South side of my new chapel which I builded lately in the parish church of Monmouth; my executors to cause a tomb of marble to be made over my grave, with images of me, Margery my first wife, and Blanch my now wife, and an epitaph to be made for me'. There was also a Milborne Chapel and a Cappers' Chapel.

But the granting of annuities and corrodies continued to impoverish the priory. Some of these were considerable. When Robert Burton retired in 1524, after only four years as prior, he was given a pension of £14 6s 0d, together with food and drink and a room in the priory.[1] This did not make things easy for his successor Richard Evesham. Even so, he soon reduced the priory to such disorder that the Duchy officials had to intervene and ask for his removal on the grounds of his 'unseemly, incontinent and unpriestly living'.

The prior had left the church unserved and allowed the buildings to decay, but it took several years for the Bishop of Hereford to act. Complaints were many. He had granted away the advowsons of local churches, signed away the tithes for seven years for £103 6s 8d, and 'absented himself from the priory for six months or more...and wandered off elsewhere'.[2] Amongst the tithes he leased were fish, fruit, saffron, onions, leeks, garlic, eggs, butter, cheese, wax, honey, flax and hemp. He was eventually deposed and replaced in 1534 by Monmouth's last prior, Richard Taylbus from Bermondsey.

By then the king had, through the Valor Ecclesiasticus, been informed of the monetary value of many monasteries. Monmouth had been found to have an income of £84 6s 8d, made up of temporalities, £20 4s 0d and spiritualities, £64 2s 8d. Charges against this were £28 4s 5d. They included

Monmouth Priory in 1815 by Thomas Tudor.

Above: The seal of Monmouth Priory.

Left: Oriel in the priory, c1490.

a pension of £10 to the vicar, leaving a net income of £56 2s 3d.[3] Taylbus did not improve on this financial position by being compelled to make further annuities including a grant to a London clothworker of £2, together with a house 'next unto Monkgate in the which dwelleth now Davy Dyar'.[4] Dyar was also given a broad cloth with 13s 4d annually for livery.

In 1536, realising what was coming, Taylbus began to disband his priory. He granted to Robert Terghwhyt, for seventy years and a rental of £6 13s 4d, 'all that mansion place lying in the town of Monmouth...joining the priory church and parish church of Monmouth, with all houses, lodgings and buildings belonging to the same, and also all their lands, meadows, pastures and underwoods, the demesne lands...' Terghwhyt paid £20 by way of fine and before signing the documents 'the said prior and convent doth acknowledge themselves well and truly contented and paid'.[5] Before this final transaction, Taylbus had disposed of most of the contents and retired to Garway. So when Dr. John Vaughan, one of Cromwell's commissioners, heard of this he wrote to his master from Brecon that, although Monmouth was not in his commission, 'there is no pot, nor pan, nor bed, nor monk in the said house, except one who boards in the town...I intend to suppress the said house for it is the voice of the people that whilst you have monks there, you shall neither have good rule nor good order'.[6]

Much of Vaughan's report must have been based on hearsay because there was a further sale of goods at the priory in February 1537. The sale included a coffer and candlesticks from the church (18d), two table boards, two forms, a cupboard, two pairs of trestles and a stained hanging from the Hall (11s 2d); a cupboard, chest and almery from the Old Buttery (3s 4d); a drape tablecloth and towel, an almery, an old chest, a pewter basin and two brass candlesticks from the Little Buttery (4s 3d); four brass pots, one brass pan, one broach, a pair of racks and two water buckets with iron chains (18s 8d) from the Kitchen; a trussed bedstead, a cupboard, a great pair of old andirons, the hanging of stained canvas, a table board, two trestles, two forms and two chairs (7s 6d) from the bishop's chamber; a hanging of stained say (woollen cloth) from the auditor's chamber (12d); and, most important, a vestment of red velvet streaked with gold (40s), an altar frontal of the same (20s), a vestment of tawny silk (10s) with two altar frontals, one of dornick (linen), the other of fustian and say (70s) and two tunicles of red velvet (6s 8d each).[7]

All the items except the vestments were bought by Thomas Williams. The Williams family, strong Catholics, were to live in the priory for many years. One tunicle was bought by the Auditor and one by Mr. Scudamore, the Receiver. The rest were bought by William Baker and William Levins. Other vestments, possibly the same, occur in the expenses of the commissioners. These include 'a certain ornament of the church delivered to the Treasurer from the Priory of Monmouth together with a velvet cope of crimson and a pallium of the colour of Baudekyn crimson valued at 100s'. There is no indication of what the 'certain ornament' was, but many details of the expenses entailed by the officials: 4s for parchment and paper, 2s 4d for money bags and 2s a day for a six-day journey to London and back.[8] In spite of these expenses a second evaluation of the priory after passing to the king (the Compoti Ministerium) gave a slightly higher income of £93 8s 9d.

When Edward VI followed his father as king in 1547 it was the turn of the chantries. In 1548/9 the chantry of St. Mary in the parish church was closed and the property supporting it was conveyed by the king to Thomas Goldsmyth. This included five houses with gardens and 42 acres of pasture and arable land scattered through Dixton and Monmouth. Goldsmyth was to hold it for twenty-one years at an annual rent of £5 13s 9d.[9] When he died it passed first to James Scudamore on the same terms, and then to Walter Spicer at a reduced rent of £4 14s 5d.

In 1547 new measures were introduced to enforce the return of any valuables remaining at large. Many churches had sold them in order to find money for the English bibles and service books which had to be used. Others must have been hidden, as were the treasures now in the Roman Catholic church in St. Mary Street. They include two beautiful mediaeval processional crosses, one of them Romanesque, and a superb chasuble, a fine example of Opus Anglicanum,[10] together with burse, chalice veil, stole and maniple. All were brought to Monmouth from Holywell in the eighteenth century.

Front view.   Back view.

Opus Anglicanum c1500 brought from Holywell and found in the Presbytery by Father Abbot who had it repaired by nuns as it had been cut into pieces to conceal it.

They had been hidden there, the chasuble having been cut up. It was reassembled and re-lined in 1837. The Romanesque cross is now in the National Museum of Wales, the rest adorn Monmouth's Roman Catholic church. There was no reference at the Reformation as to what happened to them. Nor is there any reference, if they still survived, to the 'relics of the Holy Cross, the sepulchre, winding sheet and other garments of Our Lord, as well as of many saints', said to be in the parish church at the end of the fourteenth century.

Cromwell's looting of the monasteries, his introduction of informers into towns and villages to report on opponents of the Reformation, and the fear of the Treason Act, led many people to lie low and let the orders, counter-orders and disorder issuing from above flow over them. When Mary Tudor came to the throne in 1553, many felt relief that the old traditions of faith, self discipline and ritual which had served the country for so long were returning.

The problem for the common man can be seen in the alterations to Cranmer's Book of Common Prayer of 1549. It was revised in 1552, abol-

Top left: St. Mary's R.C. Romanesque processional cross, now in the National Museum of Wales.

Top right: Fourteenth century processional cross in St. Mary's Roman Catholic Church.

Right: Wooden crucifix with linen loin cloth and hinged arms at the shoulder for use when placing the body in an Easter sepulchre. The hands badly damaged. Possibly seventeenth century Spanish.

ished by Mary in 1553, reinstated by Elizabeth in 1559, amended by James I in 1604, abolished by the Long Parliament in 1645, brought back by Charles II in 1660 and authorised at last in 1662. The twentieth century has seen the process continue and add to the confusion.

Mary reigned for only five years and parishes were faced with the problem of replacing vestments which they had been obliged to sell. Under Elizabeth change continued. Mary's roods were replaced by Elizabethan royal arms;[11] wooden communion tables supplanted stone altars, some of which were used to pave the porch as at Penallt or for salting stones as at Abbey Dore; communion cups took the place of chalices in 1571 though it took Monmouth many years to comply with this order; the screens which had concealed the mysteries of the faith were removed; English replaced Latin; and the classic Anglican concept of an auditory church with three parts, for baptism, preaching and communion began to take shape. Yet, as late as 1590 William Perkins could still write that he thought most people were papist at heart, and that it is 'safer to doe in religion as most doe'.

The last Prior of Monmouth certainly played safe. While continuing to enjoy the pension of £9 he had been granted in 1539, Richard Taylbus managed to become curate of the church of St. Thomas at Overmonnow, for which he was paid £5. He continued to live in Monmouth, where he owned a house and garden, long after his dismissal and flight to Garway.

As Elizabeth's reign drew to a close reconciliation was abroad and she could say of the 4th Earl of Worcester that he reconciled what she believed to be inconsistent, a stiff Papist and a good subject. She forgave his faith which was Popish and honoured his faithfulness which was Roman.

One of the more important effects of the closure of the priory was that the prior's rights, as rector of appropriated parishes, could be sold to laymen. Lay rectors then became responsible for the maintenance of the chancel; vicars and parishioners for the care of the nave. This could lead to trouble and in 1862 Miss Griffin, Lay Rector of Dixton, brought an action against her vicar for trespass in her chancel.[12]

The rectory in Monmouth was leased to John Collyns in 1543 and in 1563 Queen Elizabeth granted it to John Spicer. She reserved for herself the advowson of Monmouth vicarage, all timber trees 'and the tithes of salmon and other fish taken and to be taken, in the waters and rivers within the parish of Monmouth'. Spicer paid a fine of £80 and a yearly rent of £22 6s 8d, and covenanted to repair the chancel. By 1582 the rectory was in the hands of Edmund Downing and Peter Ashton who paid £13 6s 8d to the vicar and £5 to the curate to take the services. They also paid 6s 8d for synodals, 17s 9d for procurations and £6 13s 4d to the Fellows of Christ's College, Cambridge in place of the 10 marks which once went to the parent abbey in France.

If one asks what the income of a parish was in the sixteenth century, Monmouth was probably typical:

	£	s	d
Tithe of Corn and Hay	15	6	8
Tithe of Monnow Mill	1	6	8
Yearly stipend from the King's Exchequer		16	8
Tithes of wool, lambs, milk, calves, etc.	3	6	8
Oblations, marriages, etc.	10	0	0
	30	16	8

Out of this the perpetual Vicar of Monmouth, John Wynstowe, received annually £10, 'the profits of the alterage'.[13]

For comparison, the income of the vicarage of Dixton, one of Monmouth Priory's parishes, was given in the same Valor Ecclesiasticus:

	£	s	d
Tithes of hay and grain there one year with another	5	19	8
Tithes of lambs and wool		16	2
Lactual Tithes		12	6
Tithes of wood		3	4
Oblations at the three usual times of the year		6	0
Other small tithes one year with another		6	8
Glebe lands there by the year		5	0
	8	9	4

Charges:

	£	s	d
To the Prior of Monmouth		18	4
Annual procurations to the Archdeacon		6	8
Annual synodals to the Commissary		1	6
	1	6	6

	£	s	d
And it is worth clearly one year with another	7	3	0
Tenth part		14	$3\frac{3}{4}$

After the Dissolution, the Vicar of Dixton continued to pay 20s rent of the tithe of the rectory there and 5s annual portions to Thomas Williams who acted as bailiff of the priory for the king.

In spite of Elizabeth's compliments to the Earl of Worcester, recusancy,

Communion Cup from St. Mary's C. of E., hall-marked 1580 with maker's mark SB with a mullet over. The finest cup in the diocese. The cover is so unlike the usual paten shape that this may have been adapted from secular use. (Now in National Museum of Wales)

Communion cup, hall-marked 1591 with maker's mark T.F. within a shield. It is engraved with a foliate design. The ring is modern.

refusal to attend the services of the church of England, had become a punishable offence by 1559. Each failure to attend on a Sunday entailed a fine of 12d. The wealthy could afford this, the humble could not. But the Act was not enforced with enthusiasm and it was probably true that in Monmouthshire at first, 'there was no mention of factions in religion'. In 1568 William Allen had established an English College at Douai to train missionaries to serve and convert his countrymen to the old faith. A large loan to fund the college was made by Thomas Somerset who had been M.P. for Monmouthshire in 1553 and was to die in the Tower. The strength of recusancy in the county was largely due to the wealth and authority of his family.

The rising of the northern earls, the excommunication of Elizabeth, and the arrival from Douai of Edmund Campion, the greatest of their missionaries, led to new restrictions. When Campion was captured, tortured and taken to the scaffold, his last words, 'If you esteem my religion treason, then am I guilty', expressed the dilemma which many recusants faced. But the gathering of the Armada led to an act in 1587 ordering the seizure of the property of any recusants who were unable to pay £20 a month for the privilege of not attending the services of the Church of England.

Although 289 Monmouthshire recusants were named as unable to pay the fine, there were none from Monmouth until 1607 when 19 names, of whom 14 were women (always the backbone of resistance movements) appeared. By then the county led the country in the number of convicted recusants per 1,000 of the population. Monmouthshire had 117 per 1,000. Lancashire was second with 112, followed by Durham with 31 and Herefordshire with 25.[14]

In 1600 the Earl of Worcester had given the Jesuits some land at the Cwm near Llanrothal. In 1622 it became the College of Saint Francis Xavier and the centre of a new Jesuit province. As a result there were few farms in the Monnow Valley which did not contain recusants living in comparative security. This lasted until the Titus Oates plot led to a raid on the Cwm and its closure. The appointment by Rome of four vicars Apostolic after the accession of James II was short-lived. It was not until 1713 that Matthew Prichard became the first regular to hold office in England since the Reformation. He was to spend the rest of his life at Perthir on the Monnow near Rockfield where the Franciscans established a novitiate. When he died in 1750 he was buried under the communion table in Rockfield Church, one of several local Catholic priests afforded this honour by the Anglican parishes where they lived.[15]

The first Catholic Relief Act in 1778 exempted Catholics from most of the old penalties, provided they took the Oath of Allegiance. Fifty-five appeared at Quarter Sessions to do so and fourteen years later a committee was set up to arrange for the establishment of a 'Publick Catholic Chapel' in Monmouth. It was opened in 1793, having to comply with the orders of the Common Council that it should not be open to the street and should not look like a chapel.

There was more opposition to dissent than there was to recusancy. An attempt to set up a Conventicle for Presbyterian Dissenters in 1709 ran into immediate opposition from the mayor. In 1790 Howell Harris and William Seward were stoned when they tried to preach outside the Shire Hall.[16] In June 1779 a meeting in Inch Lane was disrupted by a group led by the usher of Monmouth School.[17] Alexander Mather was assaulted when trying to open a meeting house in 1771.[18] John Wesley came expecting trouble but stayed with a magistrate and left Monmouth praising its 'affectionate people'.[19] George Whitefield and his Calvinistic Methodists were less welcome but in 1818 a small Baptist Chapel opened between Monnow Street and the Monnow.[20] George Maddox, an unbeliever, built the delightful Methodist Chapel in 1837[21] and the most impressive of the chapels, the Congregational, opened in 1852.[22] The Primitive Methodist chapel in Monnow Street was designed by the pastor, George Dobson, in 1864.[23] By the time of the religious census in 1852 there were seven nonconformist meeting places with a combined congregation of 1287 adults and 137 children. The number attending Anglican services on that day was 1734 adults and 379 children. In that same census the Roman Catholics numbered 180.

2 The County of Monmouth

While the priory was being closed the authorities were turning their attention to lawlessness in Wales. From their beginnings the Marcher lords had ruled by the sword. The number of such lordships, each with its own courts, meant that it was comparatively simple for felons to escape punishment by moving from one lordship to another. Sir Edward Croft had appealed to Cromwell 'for some man to be sent down to us to use the sword of justice where he shall see cause throughout the Principality; otherwise the Welsh will wax so wild it will not be easy to bring them to order again'.[24]

Bishop Rowland Lee, chosen to carry out the task, was in Monmouth three months after John Vaughan had written his report on the state of the priory. As Lord President of the Council of the Marches he was quite ready to shed blood to restore order. He met with opposition but waived it aside, remarking that having 'hanged four of the best blood in Shropshire' he was ready to do the same in Monmouth. He found the Welsh language a hindrance to his administration so the ap was dropped and ap Robert became Probert, ap Howell - Powell , and ap Richard - Prichard. At the same time English Christian names became Welsh surnames such as Williams, Thomas, Hughes and Davies.

Lee was seeking a new headquarters for his council and suggested that if Monmouth Castle was rebuilt out of stone and wood from the priory it would be suitable[25], but nothing happened and the council chose Ludlow. He suggested Monmouth because he knew it was to become a county town. This materialised with the passing of the Act of Union in 1536.[26]

The full title was 'An Act for Laws and Justice to be ministered in Wales in like fourme as it is in this Realme'. This was to be done by joining the Marcher lordships to the shires of England or Wales, while the residue 'shall be severed and devyded into certain particular counties or shires'. The new shires were Monmouth, Brecknock, Radnor, Montgomery and Denbigh in that order.

The county of Monmouth was then defined by 'the lordshippes, townshippes, parisshes, commotes and cantredes of Monmouth, Chepstow, Matherne, Lanmyhangel, Magour, Goldcliffe, Newporte, Wenloge, Llanwerne, Caerleon, Uske, Trelecke, Tyntern, Skynfreth, Grousmonte, White Castell, Raglan, Calicote, Byston, Abergevenny, Penrose, Grenefeld, Maghen and Hothnyslade...and that the said Towne of Monmouthe shall be named accepted reputed used had and taken heed and Shire Towne of the said Countie...and that the Shire Court of the said countie shall be holden...one tyme at the said Towne of Monmouthe and next tyme at the towne of Newport'.

There were to be two Members of Parliament for the county and one for the town. The borough member was to be elected by the burgesses of Monmouth, but his expenses were to be shared by the burgesses of Usk, Caerleon, Abergavenny, Newport and Chepstow in spite of the fact that they had no vote. This taxation without representation enraged them and they refused to pay. As a result their bailiffs were summoned before the Court of Chancery for non-payment of £15 16s 8d, the cost of Thomas Kynnyllin attending Parliament from 1538 to 1544. It remained a source of resentment until 1680 when the burgesses of Newport and Usk were allowed to vote.[27]

The County seats were usually monopolised by Somersets and Morgans. But in 1572 William Morgan, who held the second seat, was opposed by Henry Herbert, the son of Thomas Herbert of Wonastow who happened in that year to be Sheriff and so responsible for the poll. Elections were usually held in the Great Hall of the Castle at 8 a.m. and by 6 o'clock on 1 May about 900 Morgan supporters assembled there to vote. Whilst waiting, there was some horseplay and a door was broken.

Meanwhile the sheriff and his son arrived at Overmonnow and, hearing the noise at the Castle, decided to hold the election at once outside the inn of Hopkin Richard. Herbert, who had most of his supporters with him, decided to take the poll by 'Shout' and read out, 'Are you content that Mr. Charles Somerset and my son Henry Herbert shall be knights of the Shire?' Some shouted 'Herbert' and some 'Somerset' but the noise carried to the castle where Morgan and his supporters immediately realised what had happened and set out at full cry down Monnow Street shouting 'Morgan'. By the time they arrived the sheriff and his son were riding at a fast gallop towards Wonastow.[28]

In spite of an appeal to the Star Chamber that the election was held before 8 o'clock and that Morgan probably had 900 supporters to Herbert's 100, Henry Herbert remained in office undisturbed as one of the members for the new county.

The other important element in the act was the exclusion of Monmouthshire from the Courts of Great Sessions which had been set up for the twelve Welsh counties. Monmouthshire, the thirteenth, was to be 'for ever...attendant to the Lord Chancellor of England, the king's justices and other of the king's council and unto all laws, customs, ordinances and statutes of this Realme of England'. This meant that Monmouth became part of the Oxford circuit. This was only one aspect of the Act's rejection of the Welsh language. All officials were forbidden to use anything but 'the Englisshe tonge'. If they disobeyed they would forfeit their office.

There was a further act in 1543 and together the two acts provided the basis for the administrative and judicial system which was to serve the county for several hundred years. The judicial regime consisted of the assizes, usually under a circuit judge, and dealing chiefly with felony. The quarter sessions, advised by the Clerk of the Peace (in 1540 it was Hugh Huntley), consisted of assembled JPs and dealt with misdemeanours and gaol delivery.

In 1542 Charles Herbert was appointed sheriff. This was an ancient office going back to the Shire Reeve. The officials below him included an escheator, two coroners and the keeper of the county gaol. Although there had been a Hundred of Hadnock in earlier days, the act of 1542 divided the county into seven new hundreds: Skenfrith (in which Monmouth was included), Raglan, Trellech, Caldicot, Usk, Newport and Abergavenny. This was convenient for militia musters and ballots, taxation and the duties of the chief constable who was appointed in 1543.

At the bottom of the judicial hierarchy were the J.P.s. They were expected to attend the assizes where they could learn the ropes and could be removed by the Privy Council if they were unsatisfactory. They could order capital punishment and where the crime was the stealing of horses this was often given. Supervision came from the Privy Council, usually by way of the Council of the Marches. Here the important figure was the lord lieutenant, given an official position in 1585.

At the base of the communal pyramid were the parishes with their wardens. In many respects they were the most effective element, eventually acquiring other officials - overseers of the poor, parish constables, surveyors of the highways and responsibility through the Vestry for roads, bridges, vagrants, the sick, the destruction of vermin, the house of correction, the poor house and the parish church.

3 The Borough

In spite of the new privileges and authority acquired by becoming the county town, all was not well there. This can be seen in the preamble to the charter which was given to the town by Edward VI in 1549. 'Taking into Our consideration how the burgesses of Our Borough and Town of Monmouth in the Marches of Wales and in our Duchy of Lancaster, have sustained not a little loss and damage, forasmuch as several profits and privileges, heretofore granted to them by...Our most renowned father, Henry the Eighth...are not only diminished but also extinguished and taken away...and therefore the town...is dissolved and discorporated'.

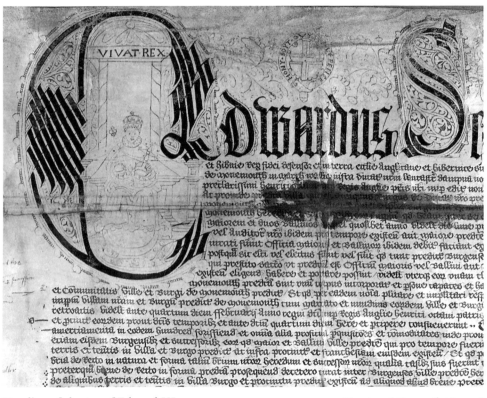

Heading of charter of Edward VI. *(Courtesy of Monmouth Museum)*

The state of the town was illustrated by the state of the castle when inspected by commissioners during Edward's reign. They found little to commend though they reported that the bridge was new made and sufficient and that the gate there was new built to the second floor with good square stones. It was covered with tile but the frame ends of the roof lay open 'whereby the Rayne fallyth into the fflore and rotteth it' so it should be mended with speed.

Everything else was deplorable. The rest of the walls, the inward buildings, both the tower's chambers, the chapel and others, saving the hall, were in great decay, 'the Roffs, Wyndowes, and Steyars pulled or fallen down and the Tyle, Tymbr, Iron and lead thereof roted'. The hall was well walled and roofed saving the east end. As this was where the assizes, quarter sessions and other courts sat, the open roof meant that 'the wynde being in the Est when men sitt there they are dreven away wt the wether'. In the same way the king's exchequer was so decayed that the auditors 'ar dreven to goe into the towne whiche we thynke moche unsemely; ffirthermore the Kyng's Gayole is wtin the forsed Gate wherefor we thynke it convenyent…the sd Gate to be made fully prfitt and fyrnyshed accordyng to the fundacions thereof'.[29]

Edward's charter added few new privileges except a fair during the week after Pentecost. It was followed in 1557 by another charter from King Philip and Queen Mary. Both are uncoloured although charters were inscribed by the donor in the hope that the recipients would decorate them. This is something Monmouth never seems to have afforded.

The purpose of Edward's charter, with its preamble about the disastrous state of the town, seems to have been to reassure any anxiety the burgesses might have over the right which the Act of Union gave to the king to dissolve a borough if he wished. There had certainly been trouble over the election of a mayor, and in 1519 it was reported to the king that there had been 'of long time great variances, strifes and debates' which had led to 'great Riots, affrays and unlawful assemblies…in the said town, both to the great unquietness and disturbance of the mayor, burgesses and inhabitants, to the great hindrance and loss of goods'.

Heading of charter of Philip and Mary.   (Courtesy of Monmouth Museum)

The remedy proposed was that the mayor and bailiffs should be elected by the twenty-five 'most honest and substantial burgesses'; but there was renewed dissension in 1537, and again in 1549, the year of Mary's charter. On this last occasion a majority of the twenty-five substantial burgesses elected Edward Cutler to be mayor, but Thomas Goldsmyth and others pointed out that three of the twenty-five were dead and then, 'using sinister and crafty information', managed to substitute 'three light persons' who, with Cutler's opponents, elected a rival mayor, William Moran. It was eventually decided that only the twenty-five select burgesses should elect a mayor. The dispute was to be repeated 300 years later in the prolonged struggle between the burgesses and the ruling oligarchy controlled by the Dukes of Beaufort between 1818 and 1835.

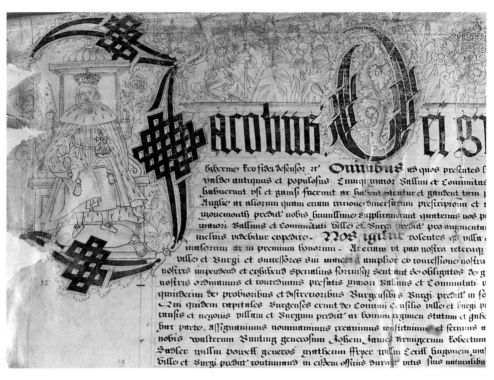

Heading of charter of James I.   (*Courtesy of Monmouth Museum*)

The charter of James I, in the form of Letters Patent, which followed in 1605 named the twenty-five chief burgesses and appointed the mayor and bailiffs to be justices of the peace for the borough. They could make ordinances in writing for governing the town and could hold land provided it did not exceed £50 a year in value. The ornamental headline contains the lion, unicorn, fleur de lis, a crowned rose and the arms of Scotland. This is the only charter on which the Great Seal is complete. It is pendant on cords of red and white silk. The remains of the seals on the Charters of Edward VI and Mary are on cords of white and green.

The new borough seal granted by Charles II in 1675.

Heading of charter of Charles II.

(Courtesy of Monmouth Museum)

The charter of Charles II, dated 18 May 1666 contains a fine portrait bust of the king with the arms of England, France, Scotland and Ireland quarterly. Each is repeated on a separate shield with the national flowers. A fragment of the seal has cords of red and white silk.

In 1703 there was trouble over where these charters should be kept, so it was agreed to use the great chest which had been given by Philip Jones in 1656. It bears that date and his initials. The borough maces were acquired in 1706.

The town chest given by Philip Jones in 1656. There were three locks, with a key for the mayor and the two bailiffs. All three had to be present to open it.*(Courtesy of Monmouth Museum)*

The borough maces, hall-marked 1706. *(Courtesy of Monmouth Museum)*

REFERENCES Part Four

(Abbreviations for some of the more frequently cited sources appear on page 8)

[1]   Regist. C. Booth, p.338.
[2]   Ibid., p.284, 287.
[3]   Other charges included £6 13s 4d to Christ's College, Cambridge and tips of from £1 to £3 to the officials.
[4]   P.R.O. E 315/100/286b. LR 1/228/29d, 30a.
[5]   Augmentation Office Roll 29, 27 Henry VIII.
[6]   Cal. State Papers, Henry VIII. X p.160.
[7]   P.R.O. C 115 Bundle D21, no. 1937.
[8]   P.R.O. Exchequer Augmentation Office. Misc. Bks. (E315) 278, f. 148.
[9]   P.R.O. DL Misc. Bks 3 Edward VI (1548/9).
[10] For the Monmouth chasuble see: Kirstie Buckland, 'The Skenfrith Cope and its Companions' in *Textile History*, 14 (2), 125-139, 1983.
[11] The Royal Arms of George II in St. Mary's were removed as 'tawdry emblems' in 1846. Dixton still has Queen Anne's.
[12] For this bizarre incident see my *Monmouth: the Making of a County Town*, pp.117-121.
[13] MBA. Transcription by Hobson Matthews of documents at P.R.O. and David Williams, 'Monmouth Priory at the Suppression, 1534-1537', *Monmouthshire Antiquary*, III, 1970-78. pp.186).
[14] F. H. Pugh, 'Monmouthshire Recusants in the reigns of Elizabeth and James' in *S.W. and Mon. Record Society*, 1957, pp.39, 63.
[15] R. W. McDonald, 'The Parish Registers of Wales' in *National Library of Wales Journal*, XIX (4), 1976, p 42.
[16] For the visit of Harris and Seward see Edgar Phillips in *Presenting Monmouthshire*, no. 10 (1960).
[17] MBA. QS Records, 25/1/1775, pp.169-172.
[18] *Wesley's Veterans*, Vol. II, p. 107.
[19] *Journal of John Wesley* (Standard Edition), vol. II, p.9.
[20] Baptist Church Register. Three men were baptised in the river.
[21] Most nineteenth century non-conformist chapels were built in classical style. This was ascribed to Pugin being both R.C. and Gothic Revivalist. See Esther Moir, 'The Architecture of Dissent', *History Today*, June 1963.
[22] The architect was Armstrong of Bristol where the Brunswick Chapel is an almost identical building by him.
[23] *Monmouthshire Merlin*, 30/4/1864.
[24] C. A. K. Skeel, *The Council of the Marches*, p.56.
[25] Cal. State Papers. Henry VIII, X. p.160.
[26] The text used is that of William Rees, *The Union of England and Wales*, 1948. Monmouth is usually spelt Mommouth.
[27] Although the borough member depended on the patronage of the Duchy, more local members served in Parliament in the sixteenth century than in any other. Kynyllin's expenses compare quite favourably with those of most current MPs.
[28] EHR. LX1, 27ff. 'More Elizabethan Elections' by Sir John Neale.
[29] MBA. Transcript of DL Special Commission, 5 Elizabeth No. 95.

Part Five
DEVELOPMENTS

1 The Militia

The defence of the realm had always been one of the major duties of a king. In c890 Alfred the Great had reorganised the peasant militia and built a system of fortresses to be garrisoned by men of the neighbourhood. The men of Archenfield had been allowed to retain their ancient customs only on condition that they gave military service. In 1181 the Assize of Arms had decreed that every man should keep weapons in accordance with his wealth. Monmouth was no exception and Giraldus in 1190 had praised the men of Gwent who 'have much experience in warfare...and are more skilled with the bow and arrow than those who come from other parts of Wales'. During these years the fortifications of the town continued to grow and in 1285 the Statute of Winchester replaced the Assize of Arms with a new emphasis on the keeping of law and order.

In 1539, after the *posse comitatus* (the power of the county) had been established, the first records of the local militia begin with the mustering of all men between the ages of 16 and 60.[1] The muster for the county has survived but the lists for Monmouth are missing. The men assembled with one or more weapons, according to their status and skills. The weapons included bows, glaythes (long two-handed swords), bills (long knives fixed to poles), saletts (helmets with adjustable visors), splints (fighting coats with metal hoops surrounding), coats of fence (reinforced fighting coats) and harness (suits of armour).

The numbers varied greatly: Caerleon produced 96 men, Tintern 17, Penalt 34, Trellech 33, Llandenny 24, Penyclawdd 3, Usk 94, Penrose 1. Sir William Morgan, Steward of Usk, Caerleon and Trellech brought himself and 40 servants upon 'geldings and round nags', while Henry Lewis of St. Pierre came with 2 demilances and 6 archers on horseback.

Henry VIII had confirmed the Statute of Winchester in 1511 and in 1558 the Muster Act placed the movement on a regular footing and organised the supply of arms. Men with an income of between £5 and £10 were to keep a coat of plated armour, a halberd, longbow and steel helmet. Those with £1000 were to provide 16 horses, 80 suits of light armour, 40 pikes, 30 longbows, 20 halberds, 20 harquebuses and 50 steel helmets. Men whose wives wore velvet kirtles or silk petticoats were to keep a light horse with appropriate equipment. Failure to muster with arms when ordered was punished by a fine of 40s or ten days in prison.

Queen Elizabeth in 1580 had appointed Sir Henry Sidney to oversee training and equipping in Monmouthshire during the Armada scare but in 1603

James I, who was accused of being unable 'to endure to see a soldier or to see men drilled; to hear of war was death to him', repealed the Muster Act of 1588, so mustering was in abeyance for nine years.

Annual general musters were reintroduced in 1612 and Charles I brought eighty-four sergeants from the Low Countries to train the Militia using exact rules. Hence what was to become known as the Exact Militia. Their stores were kept in Monmouth Castle but at the outbreak of the Civil War, when doubts about Monmouth's loyalty to Parliament which controlled the Militia were evident, orders were given that the stores be removed to Newport. Although the mayor and magistrates protested and some were imprisoned, the stores were removed.

In 1662 Charles II introduced new Militia Acts, enforcing fourteen days training, supervision by parish constables and use for general peace-keeping duties. By 1684, the Duke of Beaufort had become the first of a long line of officers from that family who were to command the local regiment until the end of the nineteenth century. As Lord President of the Council of the Marches, the Duke toured the Welsh militias in 1684, ending in Monmouth where he inspected the local regiment from a stand of pikes and watched 'Doublings, Countermarches, Wheelings, Variety of Exercises, and Good and Close fireings'. He was then given the Freedom of Monmouth and after a cold collation in the town hall, the militia gave several volleys, 'and the troops were treated as they were mounted with Syder and ye noted Monmouth Ale, Drums beating, Trumpets sounding and Bells ringing'.[2] The local militia then consisted of a regiment of foot and a troop of horse.

During the Duke of Monmouth's rebellion the regiment was stationed in Bristol to put down riots. In 1686 the first official drill book for infantry was published. The militia was called out in 1715 and 1745 for the Jacobite rebellions but in 1757 a complete reorganisation of the force took place. The men were to be raised by ballot and number 31,800. Each county was given a quota of men between 18 and 50. The lords lieutenant were to divide the specified number between parishes whose officials would control the ballot. Men were to train annually and serve for three years. Service could be avoided by paying a fine or finding a substitute. As service was not popular, substitutes were sought and in 1803, when the threat from France was evident, 90% of the 45,000 men mustered were substitutes. By then training was taking place with regular troops at huge camps like Warley, Coxheath and Rodborough. Meanwhile the Monmouth Militia had been merged with the Brecon in 1794.[3]

As the threat from Napoleon disappeared the militia was rarely mustered though in 1820 it had been renamed The Royal Monmouthshire Militia. Officers usually joined the militia as a step in the ladder of society, their rank on joining depending on income. When Colonel Morgan Clifford took command in 1846, he complained that he had inherited 'an Adjutant, four sergeants, three superannuated captains and two very questionable subalterns'.[4] Four years later the Militia Act revived the militia which had not trained for

Monmouth Militia.
SUB-DIVISION.

Hundred of *Skenfrith Lower Division*

To *Joseph Coates Castle Bayley Ward Grosmonger*

Notice is hereby given unto you,

That you are chosen, by Lot, to serve in the Militia of the County of Monmouth, and that you are to appear at the House of *Charles*

Powell # # # # Victualler, at *Lands ... Grosmonny*

in the said County, on *Thursday* # # #

the *Twentieth* # # Day of *March Instant*

~~next~~, before the Deputy Lieutenants and Justices of the Peace, to be then and there assembled, to take the Oath in that behalf required; and to be Enrolled to serve in the Militia of the said County, as a Private Militia Man, for the space of Five Years; or otherwise to provide a fit Person, to be then and there approved by the Deputy Lieutenants and Justices, who shall take the said Oath, and be then and there Enrolled as aforesaid.

Given under my Hand the *10th*

Day of *March* — — — in the Year of

our Lord 1817 — — *John Charles*

... Casling Constable of *Castle Bayley Ward*

A militia ballot paper, 1817.

twenty years. Colonel Morgan Clifford raised 300 volunteers, and appointed Major J. F. Vaughan of Courtfield, the father of the future cardinal, to be lieutenant colonel. The regiment was then renamed The Royal Monmouthshire (Light Infantry) Militia.

In 1854 Vaughan persuaded the officers to offer the regiment and £5000 for service in the Crimea. The offer was refused by Palmerston and as a result Vaughan went out on his own as supernumerary colonel. Many drafts were sent from Monmouth to the Royal Welsh Fusiliers but the headquarters of the regiment stayed at home.

On his return Colonel Vaughan published anonymously *The Soldier in Peace and War*, a far-sighted indictment of the inefficiency with which the war was being conducted.[5] While Vaughan was outside Sebastopol, Tolstoy, a young lieutenant, was inside. When the war ended Tolstoy wrote *Sebastopol Sketches*, the forerunner of *War and Peace*. Both men believed that if they had been commanded by French officers they would have won.

In 1877, under the Cardwell Reforms the militia was converted to engineers[6] and acquired the title of The Royal Monmouthshire Engineers (Militia) with Colonel Vaughan in command. He was a devout Roman Catholic and under his guidance the regiment became known as The Pope's Own. The Roman Catholic Church in Monmouth contains many items (Confessional, Baptistry tiles, Sanctuary lamp) showing its close links with the regiment which in 1896 was renamed The Royal Monmouthshire Royal Engineers (Militia), the only regiment with two Royals in its name. Two companies served in the South African War and in 1908 the militia became, officially what it had often been in fact, The Special Reserve (for the regular army). As such it served in two world wars and has been given the freedom of Monmouth, Smethwick and Swansea.

2 Schools and Literacy

Until printing was invented the chances of having something to read were remote. Monks and the wealthy would have access to manuscripts but the average Christian would be confined to the texts on the walls of his church or on monuments. What books there were lived in almeries. There were two of these in the priory at the Dissolution. Elsewhere books were chained. This was because it was said that in the Middle Ages a book was worth as much as a farm and could be much more easily stolen. There were also carrels, openings under cover where books taken from almeries could be read in a good light. There are several examples of these at Gloucester. The original library in Hereford Cathedral is said to have been founded as a muniment room by Bishop Aquablanca in 1268, over a hundred years after Monmouth Castle had been renowned for its library.

Before the thirteenth century small single volume Bibles were unknown. But in Paris the Latin Bible was redesigned for the private reader and the idea soon spread to Britain. One of the most notable has been the Tintern Bible, consisting of 339 leaves containing 65 lines in double columns. It had decorative initials, was probably written by two scribes, and is now in the National Library of Wales. It dates from the third quarter of the thirteenth century.[7]

Henry of Grosmont's *Livre de Seyntz Medicines* was written in French, but some of Henry V's letters were written in English. Possibly the oldest surviving example of local written English is in the accounts of John Cok, Bailiff to William Herbert, in 1463. They are concerned with buildings and work in Monmouth and Wyesham and are easy to understand: 'also paied for a borde to amende a dore in Sent Mary Strete and hire and nailez, iiid...also paied for wrytyng of all manere parcell wreton at divers tymes this same yere, iiis iiiid'.[8]

When Cranmer visited Hereford in 1528 he advised the local clergy that 'none of you shall discourage any layman from the reading of the Bible in English or Latin but encourage them'. So the Bible in English, and in 1588 in Welsh, became the books from which most people learned to read, often in Sunday Schools in the churches, usually the only places other than their homes where this could happen. Even in Wales Humfrey Llwydd in 1568 could write 'You shall find but few of the ruder sort which cannot read and write their own name, and play on the harp after their manner'.

The incentive to establish grammar schools was usually religious, especially if, as in Monmouth, the benefactor had strong evangelical ideas. William Jones, probably from Naas near Lydney, was a freeman of the livery of Haberdashers when he left in his will £9,000 to that company, to 'ordaine a Preacher, a Free School and Almes-houses for twenty poor and old distressed people, as blind and lame...of the Town of Monmouth where it shall be bestowed'.[9]

Jones was a Puritan and the priority given to the preacher illustrates his

A Catalogue of the Books belonging to the Free Grammar School, Monmouth (taken by The Revd. Willm. Jones Octr. 1823.

Folio Shelf A.

Staterni Ephemides
Johnson's Dictionary 2 Vols
Chamber's Dictionary 2 Vol.
Waldrons Works
Monfaucons Antiquities 6 Vol.
Camdens Britt per Gibson 2 Vol.
Hanleys Lives of the Philosophers
Erasmi Adagia
Scapulæ Lexicon
Euripidis Tragœdiæ per Barnes
Ovid's Metamorphosis per Sandys
History of England
Cambridge Verses
Maloratus in Novum Testamentum
Stowes Annals

Folio Shelf B

Holiokes Dictionary
Calipini Dictionarium 2 Vol.
Concordantia Bibliorum Latinorum.
Aristotelis Opera 1. Vol.
Dr. Hammond's Works Vol. 1st.
Hebrew & Latin Bible
Per Eusebium Latina Historia Ecclesiæ
[illegible]

Aretius in Novum Testamentum
Moll's Geography
Leighs Critica Sacra
Juvenal ab Hennico
Amphitheatrum
Geography 1 Vol.
Thesaurius Linguæ Romanæ et Brittanicæ
Andernacus Utilitate Imitationis.

Folio Shelf N.

Lhuyds Archæologia Brittanica 1 Vol.
Commentia in Mosew a Lapide
Horatii Opera per Caboticum
Fulke in Novum Testamentum
Musculus in Genesin
Herocleti Historia
Nicholas Machiavel
Servius Virgilius
Chillingworte
Calvin in Psalma
Jewels reply to Harding
Trapps Virgil 1. Vol.
Whites reply to Fisher
Helvici Chronologia
Leonidas

First page of a catalogue of books in Monmouth School library in 1823.

concern to convert an area in the Marches which was still, when the school opened in 1614, strongly recusant. His munificence was slightly tarnished by the Haberdashers changing Free School to Free Grammar School and then charging admission. There were also objections by the townspeople to the supremacy of Latin, but they were gradually overcome. Latin's continuing importance can be seen in any page of the school library catalogue of 1828, while the headings of the Borough Council minutes did not change from Latin to English until 2 July 1803. Quarter Sessions made the same change in 1833.

With the later additions of the high school for girls in 1892 and the Jones Endowed School in 1906, teaching soon became Monmouth's chief occupation. Meanwhile reading had been taught to the young by governesses, by the SPCK, by church schools, and by private academies, so that by the mid-nineteenth century there were few children in Monmouth who could not read something.

3 Prosperity

Monmouth depended on its market and the market in turn depended on the produce of the land and free passage on the Wye. An enquiry held by Duchy officials into the acreage of the fields took place in 1563.[10] They heard John Byrley, aged 70, describe them in detail. The commissioners were then told the names of the occupants.

Chyppyngham contained 40 acres and was occupied by thirteen tenants, one of whom owned the Butt Acre where archers were compelled to practice. (This lay between the garden of Cornwall House and Lloyd's Bank).

Williamsfield contained 40 acres 'and more' and was occupied by nine men.

Castel field contained 80 acres which included 3 acres of the Barber's Meadow and 5 acres of Colmanmede, and was held by twenty-four occupants

Dyxton field contained 18 acres and had four occupants.

Warrtreham (in front of Troy House) contained 60 acres and more, but was held by only two men.

Poleham contained 12 acres and had one tenant.

Depeham had 30 acres and one tenant.

Badypitt (Baileypit) contained 80 acres and more, and held three tenants.

King's Leyes was 17 acres and had one tenant.

It was from these fields that much of the produce sold in the market came. Many old Welsh land measures continued to be used well into the eighteenth century even by the dukes of Beaufort. A map of the Troy estate, dated 1712 states 'some distance around the town of Monmouth the customary land measure is covers, of which 3 make 2 acres'. On this basis the Troy estate comprised 1058 'neate covers' (about 704 acres) valued at £483 4s 10d. The cover is an anglicised form of the Welsh ploughing measure, the cyfar.[11] There are still many fields around Monmouth such as Six Covers and Twelve Covers, for instance, which measure 4 acres and 8 acres respectively.

The cattle and sheep markets were originally held in Monnow Street, wide down the middle and gated at each end so that animals could not escape. That splendid prospect has recently been erased by tasteless paving and parking additions. Produce, like grain and butter, was sold in front of the houses along the street.

The court house in the Market Square was built by Philip Jones of Treowen in 1571 on the site of an earlier building. Jones appointed Thomas Kerver and John Morys to build it within a year at a cost of £44. It was 70 feet long and 20 feet wide with eight stone pillars and four great windows of eight to ten lights. Jones provided and transported the timber and the builders were to remove the stone and roofing of the old building and with it build a school at the end of St. Thomas's church at Overmonnow. The new Court House was to contain 'a fair board in manner of a chequer with benches and forms handsomely and decently for the mayor and bailiffs...and others their brothers to sit and keep court'.[12] There is no mention in the contract of a market until Mr. Jones 'took [the mayor] by the hand and told him...that he sorrowed to see the country people stand with their grain in the wet open street'. At a meeting in 1652 a number of farmers came to Monmouth to complain about the move to the court house. When they sold corn in the street they paid no toll but the owners of the houses before which they stood swept the pavement and sold the sweepings at a profit. When they were forced back to the court house it was done with violence by a soldier called Bond, 'a runagate fellow' who had petitioned the Commissioners for Pious Uses. It was said that he bore malice to the owners of the houses. But when corn was sold at the court house a portion of corn was taken in a brasen dish as a toll.

The town's Elizabethan bushel measure inscribed ELIZABETH DEI GRACIA ANGLIÆ FRANCIÆ ET HIBERNIÆ REGINA 1601.

In an attempt to appease the farmers it was decided to give the corn to the poor, but few people believed this and the farmers went back to the street. No plan of this first court house has survived but an impression, based on the contract, has been made by Mr. F. C. Bowler, A.R.I.B.A.[13]

That building was not satisfactory as a market, nor were the assizes held there, but it did provide a building where the council could assemble and

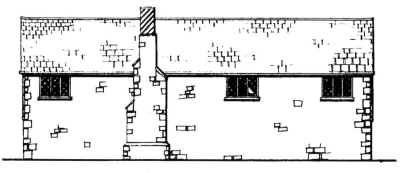

SOUTH ELEVATION.

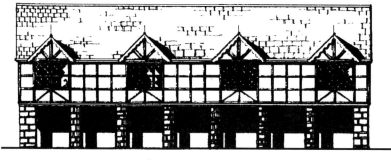

NORTH ELEVATION.

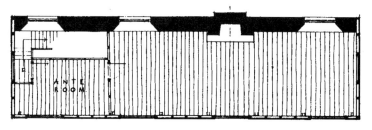

PLAN OF COURT HOUSE.

Monmouth Court House and Market Hall 1571. Reconstruction drawing as made from specification dated 1571. F. C. Bowler, A.R.I.B.A.

where the local magistrates could administer justice. The assizes were held in the great hall of the castle until complaints about the leaking roof led to their transfer c1700 to Great Castle House. This had been built by the third Marquess of Worcester in 1673 as a town house while he was building at Badminton and Troy House.[14]

The county magistrates decided that a purpose-built court was needed and, in 1723, decided to pull down the 1571 building and erect one suitable for both assizes and quarter sessions. William Rea and Edward Catchmayd agreed, for the sum of £1700, to take down so much of the old building as was necessary and 'build a convenient, strong and handsome market house and two courts of judicature and also a room proper and convenient for the use of the Grand Jury at Assizes and Sessions, and of the mayor, etc. at all other times, with a table and fire hearth'. The cost of the building was to be shared between the county paying £1600 and the corporation £100.[15]

The building which opened in 1724 had problems. In 1743 the corporation sent a petition to the Duke of Beaufort asking him 'of his bounty to supply a large expense for the repair of the town hall...being very much decayed'.[16] There is no evidence that the duke responded, but Philip Hardwick, a Bristol carpenter, agreed to repair the arches on the ground floor for £385. The original architect was said by a previous town clerk to have been Philip Fisher of Bristol. It seems that Hardwick was a friend as they have a joint memorial in St. Mary's church.[17]

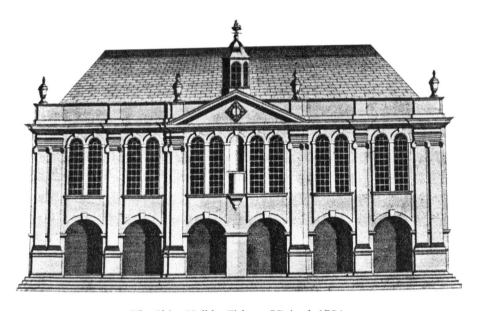

The Shire Hall by Fisher of Bristol, 1724.

In 1821 there were new problems and a committee was appointed to discuss the rebuilding necessary to make it more suitable for the assizes. Delay by the corporation led the county magistrates to approach the Duke of Beaufort with plans for a new Assize Court near Great Castle House. A print of the proposed building has survived. It was probably sufficient to make all those engaged drop the idea and apply for a Monmouth County Hall Act to enlarge the existing building.[18] This received the Royal Assent in 1829; the building to be vested in the county but certain rooms to be reserved for the corporation. The architect chosen was Edward Haycock who was then working at Clytha Park. A new staircase, larger courts and an extension at the back along Agincourt Street were the chief improvements; the produce market was to be removed to a new building but the sale of corn, flour, wool and hops was to remain under the arches. It was opened in 1831 for the assizes, the cost being £6,876 7s 4d. for the building, £143 for furnishing and £467 6s 6d for the Act of Parliament.[19]

The Shire Hall in 1850 after restoration by Edward Haycock

The emphasis on the comfort of the judges in the Shire Hall meant that a more suitable place was needed for the produce market. This coincided with an outcry against the use of Church Street by the mail coaches. They had to travel at full gallop and there were many accidents. So when the formidable Mrs. Syner, a gingerbread maker who lived in the street, was run over, she organised a petition for a by-pass.[20] A prize of £10 was offered for the best solution. It was won by George Vaughan Maddox, a local builder who proposed a viaduct from the Bull Ring to the Hereford Road resting on twenty-six slaughter houses. It meant the removal of a group of inns and houses on the steep slope going down from the priory to the Monnow, the erection of a new market hall between the road and the castle, and the re-facing of the houses on the south side of the new street.[21] In spite of many set-backs this fine groups of buildings was opened in 1839, a valuable addition to the town's amenities and a far better scheme than that of the Ministry of Transport over a hundred years later when, with the A40, they brutally severed Monmouth from the river on which it had depended for over two thousand years.

THE RIVER

The basic necessities of life came from the surrounding farms and fields; luxuries came up the river from Bristol and Chepstow. So it was important to keep the Wye clear of obstructions like weirs. They had been a trouble in the thirteenth century when the Abbot of Tintern built one which had to be destroyed by officials from Monmouth. In 1622 the complaints came from higher

131

up stream and Monmouth weir was the cause of trouble.

The Commissioner of Sewers arrived and interviewed a group of Monmouth boatmen whose average age was about 90.[22] They all agreed that Monmouth weir had been there a long time and caused no interference. William Roberts, aged 85, remembered the weir being built at the end of Queen Mary's reign and that there were no through boats under Monmouth Bridge. 'Wines were brought from Bristol to Monmouth and unladened below the bridge and then carried by wain to Hereford. Boats were drawn by line by men up the river to Monmouth from Brockweir'.

William Bedowe, aged 90, said the weir was built on the foundations of an ancient one. He confirmed that the Wye was navigable for 'woodbushes' (rafts) and long trows from Severn to Brockweir 'whence they are drawn by line...with great pain and labour'.[23] James Traherne, aged 92, from Dixton remembered the weir being built, while Philip Tanner, a fisherman, had seen timber being carried from Whitchurch to Lydbrook in small boats and 'cocks'.

The weir in question belonged to Benedict Hall, and was 11 feet high on a foundation of loose stones 'with cubbs of stakes and boughs of trees platted together to stay the stones there; upon this loose, confused stone there is raised a hedge with many great stakes and small poles of about five feet high above the stone'.[24] It was said to be quite impassable to large boats which had to be dragged by teams of oxen overland. The owners complained that their boats were damaged because they were deliberately dragged over rough rocks where local carpenters waited ready, at a cost, to repair them.

The commissioners found that it was dangerous to small boats, and caused a scarcity of salmon because of the many traps attached to it which caught the fish out of season. They said that the weir should be destroyed and the channel cleared of wood and stones. The owner appealed and it was not until the eighteenth century that it was removed.

One of the Commissioners of Sewers was Rowland Vaughan who wrote in 1610, 'Take pitty on a whole country groaning under the burthen of intollerable weares...the river of Wye...was...so Weared and fortified as if the salmon therein (on paine of imprisonment) had been forbidden their usual walkes'. He had seen the river at Chepstow 'swollen with a sea of salmon' and claimed that until weirs restricted their movement, 'a Herefordshire servant would surfeit on fresh salmon as oft as a Northamptonshire man on fatt venison'.[25]

Attempts to remove the weirs continued throughout the seventeenth century. In 1697 Daniel Denell wrote a report for the Trustees of the Wye and Lugg on the state of the rivers. He had been commissioned to accompany three boatmen on a survey of the whole length and to estimate the cost of removing all obstructions. They were three days and two nights on the task, the boatmen being paid £2 2s 10d and Mr. Denell £1 2s 0d. His description of Monmouth weir shows that it had remained unchanged except that the nine fishtraps were catching even more fish. It was estimated that the removal of the weir would cost £100 but, when it was eventually destroyed, the

Marquess of Worcester who had acquired it received £1200 in compensation.[26]

Monmouth's point of view remained unchanged throughout the centuries; the river should be free of obstructions downstream to Chepstow so that the town's trade with Bristol and beyond could be kept free. Above Wye Bridge it was up to Hereford and Ross to clear the river if they wanted to.

4 Industry

What the boats carried varied, but over the years wine seems to have predominated. Heavier loads included the church bells which were usually made at Gloucester, brought down the Severn to Chepstow, and then dragged upstream by bow-hauliers, even as far as Hay-on-Wye. Wine was for the wealthy. Ale and mead were for the common man. Both were produced locally. Mead came from honey and not all the honey paid in rent in the eleventh century was to provide wax for the candles at the Mass. In spite of the levy of 17 gallons of ale for every brew of ale for sale in the fourteenth century, brew houses abounded. A typical one in Monnow Street in 1583 belonged to Moore Gwyllym, the mayor, and contained:

Imprimis twoe fornesses price three pounds.
Item twoe greate vates price twenty shillings
Item twoe yelding Vates and twoe watering tubs price ten shillings.
Item fowretene Betchinges price fowretene shillings.
Items twoe Bonnys price twelfe pens.
Item twoe Chornes price twoe shillings.
Item one hearseeve and two cowles price twoe shillings.
Total £5 9s 0d[27]

Henry VII in 1495 authorised magistrates to control ale houses where necessary. The chief reason at the time was to prevent the population from being distracted from the butts where they were expected to practise archery. Thirty years earlier George Ashby had stressed to his prince the importance of archery:

> By lawe every man shold be compellede
> To use the bowe and shotynge for disport...
> And eche towne to have Buttes for resort
> Of every creature for their comfort.

By 1552 all innkeepers had to be licensed. Even so, vast quantities of ale were consumed, encouraged by the practice of many farmers paying their labourers in ale. As a result the Privy Council, through the Council in the Marches, sent a directive to Monmouthshire complaining of the continuing surfeit of alehouses whereby, 'felons are increased, thieves, murderers and women of light conversation are harboured, rogues and vagabonds maintained, whoredom and dettestable life, unlawful games as - Dice, Cards, Bowls, Kayles [Ninepins], Quoits - commonly exercised'. Few attempts by the Elizabethans to restrict drinking were successful; one that was doomed from the start was the decree that 'tippling' in any alehouse should not last for more than one hour.[28]

Lack of success in Monmouth can be seen by the number of inns the town could support over the succeeding centuries. Few mayors set any great standard of restraint. The mayor's annual dinner in 1773, for example, managed to get through 112 gallons of ale at 2s a gallon as well as a mountain of food. (See appendix G)

Fifty years earlier than this banquet there were 85 alehouses in the town distributed as follows:

5 in Wyesham
11 in Overmonnow
23 in Wyebridge Ward
22 in Monnow Street Ward
24 in Castle Bailey Ward.[29]

In 1851 there was a reduction to 82 which included 15 beer shops. This meant that there was one inn for every 73 inhabitants. In 1901 a national survey of the drinking habits of the nation found that there were only three towns in Britain with fewer than 100 people to an inn. By dividing the number of inns into the local population a table was constructed which was led by Monmouth and followed by Bridport and Lichfield.[30]

Town	Inns	Population	Average per inn
Monmouth	61	5095	83.52 men, women, children
Bridport	64	5941	92.87
Lichfield	81	7912	97.50

The average for the whole country was 242. Nelson in Lancashire received especial praise for having 1,093 crammed into each of its few bars. These statistics coincided with others showing the number of crimes committed by each thousand persons in every county. Again Monmouthshire came top with 339 per 1000, Glamorgan second with 257 and London third with 218.

These statistics appeared at a time when Disestablishment and Sunday closing were causing Anglo-Welsh argument and their compiler ended his report accusingly with the remark that Monmouth was confirmed 'as the capital of by far the most criminal county. It stands by itself and until it is reformed it need not expect any more contention for the doubtful honour of its inclusion in either England or Wales'.

Superficially the inhabitant's chief occupations have been as boatmen on the river, as teachers of children, as participants in the market, and as the brewers and sellers of ale. But this would be disingenuous. Excavation by the Monmouth Archaeological Society has revealed that industry, as well as farming and drinking, flourished. Amongst the trades that have been uncovered are leatherworking[31], bell-founding[32], tile making and decoration[33], a wide range of pottery[34] and forges and furnaces.[35] And, as industry increased on the lower Wye, Monmouth became a dormitory town for the managers and owners, while local carpenters began building ships of considerable size

135

on the river banks.

The making of Monmouth caps was a cottage industry which flourished in Monmouth and many other towns in the sixteenth century. The cap was a plain, woollen affair not unlike the so-called Phrygian cap covering the heads of the warriors carved by the Herefordshire school of Romanesque sculptors in the twelfth century. It resembled a tea cosy and was worn by civilian and soldier alike.

In 1550 there is an early reference in the Hundred Court 'ad artem de knytting de Cappes'.[36] When the town charters were lost in 1561 they were found being used by Thomas Capper instead of a cloth under his caps in his shop window. In 1576 Richard Talbot of Goodrich sent his father a New Year's gift of 'a Monmouth Cappe, a rundlette of perrye, and...a pair of Rosse boots'.[37] In 1627 the Privy Council had ordered '6,000 suits for land soldiers, viz. cassacks, hose, cloath, shoes, stockings, shirts, bands and Monmouth caps'.[38] Cromwell equipped his army with them, bought in Bewdley for 23s a dozen and in 1662 prospective emigrants to America were advised to spend 1s 10d on one as a priority.[39] By then there had been a Cappers' Chapel in St. Mary's for some time, considered by Thomas Fuller 'better carved and gilded than any other part of the church'.[40] The navy included them in its list of slop clothing at 2s 6d each, though citizens knitting at home charged only 2d a cap. Shakespeare wrote Henry V in 1599 and makes Fluellen refer to Welshmen wearing leeks in their Monmouth caps at Crecy. It is doubtful whether they were in use at either Crecy or Agincourt but there was a Thomas Capper in the retinue of the Duke of Gloucester at the latter battle.[41] By the end of the seventeenth century their shape was changing and they were beginning to look like a grenadier cap.

So what of the three heads still staring earnestly from the wall of the priory? The lordship had passed from the king to the Somerset family when the Earl of Worcester bought it, with the castle, for £400 in 1631. The borough continued to control the town with its limited resources until reorganisation in this century transformed four ancient boroughs into the unsatisfactorily named Borough of Monmouth. The town council remains, weakened but waiting to be strengthened in the current upheaval. Only the parishes are largely unchanged, functioning in peaceful co-operation; Monmouth, Dixton, and Overmonnow, Nonconformists and Roman Catholics alike; in many respects a return to the Roman parochia, a community dwelling together in Christian unity.

Until the mid-nineteenth century many aspects of the Middle Ages would have been familiar to those three heads. Sanitation was still non-existent. The streets were filthy. Men continued to be stripped to the waist and flogged at the cart's tail. Women were expected to behave better than men, so when in 1856 two men and two girls were taken to court for immoral behaviour, the girls each received two months hard labour and the men were told not to do it again. Public transport was rare and uncomfortable. The churchyard was raised high above the streets by accumulating corpses. In spite of the amount of ale consumed, water was still the most dangerous drink, as the water cart was filled a few yards below the entry of the town drain into the river. Most wells received their water from springs in the churchyard. Animals continued to be slaughtered in Butchers' Row (Church Street). Huge crowds gathered to watch men being hanged from the gallows on the roof of the county gaol. Bulls and badgers were publicly baited in the Bull Ring. Teeth were extracted by the blacksmith and amputations were performed without anaesthetics. Surgeons were paid in kind, and O. G. Thomas in 1835 received fifty-six pairs of boots for 9 guineas worth of medical treatment. The lot of the common soldier was to be little better in the Crimea and First World War than it was at Agincourt; children coming from school terrorised the streets and crime flourished.

But within the first years of the eighteenth century, the Shire Hall had been erected and St. Mary's Church rebuilt. By then the Duke of Beaufort's

The River Monnow from Priory Street.

houses at Troy and the Castle were setting standards where local craftsmen could gain experience and builders and architects discover the latest building styles. Above all, Monmouth was to become the home of the Maddox family, builders and architects who were to provide in Priory Street the finest viaduct and by-pass Monmouth has ever had, together with many of the houses which still distinguish its streets from those of most other towns.

Thomas Churchyard had described Monmouth in 1587 as:

> A trim shire town for noble baron or knight
> A cittie sure, as free as is the best,
> Where Size is kept, and learned lawyers rest;
> Bright, Auncient, Wise, in sweete and wholesome ayre,
> Where the best sort of people ofte repayre.

He was probably overstating his case at the time. But what would those three bewildered heads, still there in the twentieth century, be thinking of Monmouth today? Provided their ears and noses were accustomed to the noise and fumes of traffic, they could still look out over Vauxhall and contemplate a river and a vale which to Thomas Gray in 1770 was the delight of his eyes and the very seat of pleasure.[42]

REFERENCES Part Five

(Abbreviations for some of the more frequently cited sources appear on page 8)

1   I am indebted to Col. John Pope for the muster roll of 1539. It is unfortunate that the Monmouth section is missing. P.R.O. E36/26 and E36/42.

2   Thomas Dineley, *The Official Progress of the first Duke of Beaufort through Wales in 1684*. Ms. at Badminton. Published in facsimile in 1888.

3   See Kissack, 'Life in the Militia, 1778-1812' in *Monmouthshire Antiquary*, VII, 1991, pp.71-81.

4   See Col. Morgan-Clifford, *Reminiscences of his Life, 1806-68*. Published privately, 1893.

5   Printed by W. Davy & Son Ltd. For Vaughan see Kissack, 'Colonel Vaughan in the Crimea 1855', Castle and Regimental Museum.

6   The change was opposed by the Duke of Beaufort, to whom all engineers were plumbers.

7   Daniel Huws, 'The Tintern Abbey Bible', in *Monmouthshire Antiquary*, VI, 1990.

8   Anthony Hopkins, 'The earliest Written English in Monmouthshire', in *Monmouthshire Antiquary*, XI, 1995.

9   See K. E. Kissack, *Monmouth School and Monmouth 1614-1995*, Lapridge, 1995.

10   MBA. Transcript of Deposition Roll 69 5 Elizabeth (1563).

11   Map of the Troy estate. Monmouth Museum.

12   Augmentation Office: Roll 29, 27 Henry VIII.

13   W. H. Baker, 'The Shire Hall' in *Presenting Monmouthshire*, no.23, Vol. II, pp.7-15.

14   The temporary use of this house, built in 1673, meant that the dividing walls between the five rooms on the first floor had to be removed to make a court room. It is now the Regimental Officers' Mess.

15   P.R.O. Assize 2/7 Crown Minute Book, 1720-1723, Oxford Circuit, Monmouth.

16 W. H. Baker, op. cit., p.11.
17 Marble tablet to Philip Fisher, d.1776 and P. Meakins Hardwick, d.1818.
18 MBA. The design was by W. Parry, a strangely castellated Gothick affair, mercifully never built.
19 W. H. Baker, op. cit., p.15.
20 *Monmouthshire Merlin*, 21/3/1835. MBA. PM 1831-40. III.
21 Kissack, *Monmouth: The Making of a County Town*, Phillimore, 1975, p.298.
22 MBA. Transcript of Depositions, 4 Oct. 1622.
23 Ibid., vol II, Monmouth Records.
24 Survey of the Wye and Lugg. BM. Additional Mss. 21567. f.3. See also Kissack, *The River Wye*, T. Dalton, 1978.
25 Rowland Vaughan, *Most Approved and Long Experienced Water-works*, 1610.
26 *A Survey of the Rivers Wye and Lugg*, 1697. See also I. Cohen, 'The Non-tidal Wye and its Navigation', in Woolhope Transactions, XXXV, pt II, 1956.
27 M.C.A. 4971.
28 Quoted by Ben Howell, *Law and Disorder in Tudor Monmouthshire*, Merton Press, 1995, p.1xxix..
29 See Kissack and Davies, *The Inns and Friendly Societies of Monmouth*, Bristol, 1981.
30 *Monmouthshire Beacon*, 12/12/1902 & 13/2/1903.
31 See S. Clarke, in *Archaeology in Wales*, vol. 33 (1993).
32 See S. Clarke, in *Archaeology in Wales*, vol. 34 (1994)
33 See S. Clarke, 'The Origins of Medieval Pottery in South-East Wales', in *Medieval Ceramics* 15, 1991, pp.29-36.
34 Ibid.
35 See S. Clarke, in Archaeology in Wales, vol. 31, 1991; vol. 33, 1993 and vol. 34, 1994, pp.69, 70. Also S. D. Coates, *The Water Powered Industries of the Lower Wye Valley*, 1992.
36 MBA. Hundred Court, 1 Edward VI, 16th January.
37 Quoted by R. Waugh in *Monmouth*, c1860.
38 Acts of the Privy Council, 2/12/1627.
39 Broadsheet in *Life in America* by M. B. Davidson, Mifflin, 1951, p.51.
40 T. Fuller, *The Worthies of England*.
41 For a full account see Kirstie Buckland, 'The Monmouth Cap' in *Costume*, vol. 13, 1979.
42 Thomas Gray to Doctor Wharton, August 1770.

Overmantle in the King's Head Inn, c1675.

Great Castle House, 1673.

St. Mary's Church by Smith of Warwick 1737.

Cornwall House garden front added in 1752.

Buildings by G.V. Maddox

Above : Kingsley House, Monk Street, c1830.   *Below* : Western facade of Priory Street, 1837.

Slaughter houses and Priory Street Viaduct, 1835.

Buildings by G.V. Maddox

Masonic Lodge, 1846.

Methodist Chapel, 1837.

APPENDIX A

THE FOUNDATION OF THE CASTLE CHURCH
1075-1083?

WITHENOC of Monmouth, to all men, his friends and neighbours, to all faithful sons of Holy mother Church, both present and future, Greetings.

Be it known unto you that I, Withenoc, being moved by divine impulse, the advice of God, and at the request of my soldiers and vassals, have built a church in my castle of Monmouth, for the Honour of God and the Holy Virgin and St. Florent, and for the health of my soul and my parents; and have granted it forever to St. Florent de Saumur, from whence I have invited monks to occupy it; and in order that they may live regularly serving God, I have granted them certain possessions in lands, in churches and in tenths namely: the church of St. Cadoc, on ground near my castle in my manor, where the monks were first accommodated before the church of Monmouth was finished; the church of St. Wingaloe; the church of Welsh Bicknor; the church of Westhope; the church of Eilida Hope with its chapel at Huntley; the church of Tibberton; the church of Stretton with its chapel at Asperton; and three carucates of land near Monmouth castle; and one carucate in Llangattock; and one carucate in Suenton; and two parts of all the tithes in my manor, whether in my possession or in the possession of my vassals, and tenths of all my mills and tenths of all my taxes. I confirm these gifts, under my seal, to remain in their possession for ever. The witnesses of this are

My brother Baderon, William Yvin, Robertus and Paganus [Baderon's sons], Ywen Trone, Raterius, Robertus Bernardi, Gulendus, Ingelerius, Hugo Bos, Randulfus de Rochevilla, Ran. de Tiberton, Salomon, Renaldus Grosus.

Endorsed: Carta Wyenoci de eccl et aliis possessionibus.

(Dugdale, *Monasticon*, IV, p.595).

APPENDIX B

DETAILS OF THE PRIORY ENDOWMENTS c1086

WITHENOC and William his nephew gave to St. Florent of Saumur the church of Monemuda and all their churches, and the tithes of all their lands and of all their tenants (homines), namely, of grain, of stock, of honey, of iron, of mills, of cheeses, and of whatever is tithed. They also gave, near the castle of Monemuda, the land of three ploughs (carrugarum) and the mill of Milebroc, and a meadow at Blakenalre, and land at St. Cadoc, and a meadow beneath their castle, and a virgate of land, namely Godric's, and at Siddington a hide of land, and in all their woods pannage for swine of (the monks') demesne. They also gave all wood required by the monks or their men for building. Lastly they granted seven burgesses in their market place, free from all toll and from all dues, save offences deserving corporal penalty.

Testes: Wihenocus sancti Florentii monachus; Rannulfus monachus; Gislebertus monachus; Petrus monachus.

De hominibus domini Willelmi: Robertus filius Bernardi; Hugo dapifer; Mainus filius Hateguis; Ivo presbiter; Mainus de Labutsac; Renaldus Grosus; Hugo Bos; Aernaldus de Villa Osberti; Raterius filius Wihenoci; Hugo Rufus; Rogerius privignus Hugonis; Rodaldus; Brientius Senex;

De famulis sancti: Robertus famulus et alii plures.

Moreover the monks notify that they are to find the lord a chaplain who will serve him properly.

The wife and the daughters of the lord William - namely Iveta and Advenia - confirmed this gift, of which confirmation the witnesses are:

Salomon et Willemus filius ejus;[1] Willelmus frater Roberti; Robertus Walensis filius Domni Willelmi; Gosfridus diaconus; Berengarius dispensator; Renaldus filius Odonis sacerdotis, et Eudo Rotator.

(Charter Roll in Archives of Maine et Loire, J. H. Round, op. cit.,p.406).

---

[1] Salomon and his son William were Bretons. The former held 4 hides in both Ruardean and Hope Mansell of William FitzBaderon. (Domesday Book)

APPENDIX C

PRIORS OF MONMOUTH

c1130	Geoffrey (Goffredus Parvus)	1398	Robert Ward
c1145	Robert	1413	William Eyton
c1240	Florentius	1433	Richard Horton
1248	Robert	1455	James Onybury
1264	William Moretau	1457	John Beynham
1297	Peter de Bosco	1464	Thomas de Lighe
1300	David de Coleville	1465	Reginald Mathon
1315	Elias	c1495	John Mydleham
1320	Ralph de Cambourne	1507	Thomas Fowler
1349	William Pipun	1520	Robert Burton
1375	John Blewyn	1524	Richard Evesham
1379	Thomas Tinney	1534	Richard Taylbus

NB I am indebted to the Reverend David Williams for many of these names.

VICARS OF MONMOUTH

1287	Ricard de Stretton	1618	Robert Brabourne
1297	John Heorl	1652	Robert Charnock
1307	Roger de Carlyon	1658	Nicholas Carey
1324	John de Horwood	1663	Charles Godwin
1349	Nicholas de Lannmorham	1677	Herbert Pye
1350	John de Leycestre	1715	Herbert Pye
1375	Richard Balle	1726	John Ollard
1379	John de Cresseny	1732	Morgan Bullock
1383	Henry Newman	1761	Richard Bellamy
1390	David Howell	1770	Richard Bellamy
1408	Philip Dygery	1772	John Davis, D.D.
1421	John Beyngton	1798	Duncombe Pyrke Davis
1422	Walter Faber	1815	Thomas Prosser
1445	John Drover	1822	Henry Barnes
1490	John Mareys	1837	George Roberts
c1495	Edward Jenyns	1846	John George Storie
1505	John Strensham	1849	Edward Francis Arney
1534	John Solas	1875	Sidney Phillips
1534	Lawrence ap Harry	1879	Wentworth Watson
1535	John Wynstone	1892	William Neville
1536	John Cole	1897	Charles Frederick Reeks
1545	Thomas Hopkyns	1912	Alfred Monahan
1547	William Hyndley	1940	Percival Knight
1563	Charles Godwin	1968	C.P. Willis
1575	Edward Threlkeld	1977	John Rogers
1576	James Powell	1984	James Coutts
1598	David Jones		

APPENDIX D

HADNOCK EXCHANGED FOR THREE IRON FORGES c1170

BADERON of Monmouth, to all men, neighbours and friends, French, English and Welsh, future and present, Greeting.

Be it known unto you that I, with the consent of my sons, Gilbert and James, have given and granted to the prior and monks of Monmouth, in exchange for Hodenac, three forges, valued at twenty shillings each, in my town of Monmouth, on the banks of the Wye, which with the iron manufactured there, shall be free from all toll, forestage and passage, and all other kinds of tax whatsoever; and also I have granted that they who buy and sell iron from the three aforesaid forges shall also be quit and free from all customs, and also free of my wharf or toll, reserving this condition, that if I shall hereafter find these three forges detrimental to me, I shall give in return for them forty shillings a year.

Besides the aforesaid agreement between myself and the monks, let there be this distinction, that so long as the charcoal used in the aforesaid forges comes from my wood, they shall be free of forestage; if from another man's wood, as far as concerns myself, they shall also be free, but pay the accustomed duty to the owner of the wood. Concerning my aforesaid wharf, buyers and sellers shall be free, but if any person shall buy iron from these forges to sell again for profit, and shall again place the iron on my wharf, he shall pay toll from thence; and whoever in my manor should wish to hold the aforesaid forges of the monks let him have free liberty, except that I grant to no person who holds a forge of me, permission to have my forge for one of the monks; and if he chooses to take both (that is one of mine and one of the monks) he may, provided he does not suffer mine to fall into decay.

This my gift I have given and confirmed under my seal in the presence of my vassals.

Witnesses for the monks: Robert the prior, Maurice, William the Cellarer.

Of the Clergy: Guidone the chaplain, Master Roger (Gilbert's secretary), Patricius the clerk, Godfrey the scribe.

Of the Laity: Gilbert, son of Baderon, James his brother, Serfel son of Dunwell, Robert de Abbetat, William son of Robert, Robert de Albermarle, Walter Marmiun, William de Mareis, cook, etc.

(Dugdale, *Monasticon*, IV, p.596).

This charter has been dealt with by Dr. H.R. Schubert in an article on 'The Mediaeval Iron works at Monmouth and Osbaston' in the Journal of the Iron and Steel Institute.

APPENDIX E

THE CHARTER OF HENRY III, 1256

HENRY, by the Grace of God, King of England, Lord of Ireland, Duke of Normandy, Aquitaine, and Count of Anjou, to his Archbishops, Bishops, Abbots, Priors, Earls, Barons, Justices, Sheriffs, Provosts, and all his Bailiffs and faithful subjects, Greeting. Know ye that we have granted and by this charter confirmed to the Burgesses and good men of Monmouth that neither they nor their goods, in whatever place in our land or dominion they be found, shall be arrested for any debt of which they are not the sureties or principal debtors, unless it happen that they are debtors of their commune, having that with which they can repay their debts, wholly or in part, and it having been reasonably shown in justice that they owe it to their creditors. And that the burgesses and good men shall not lose their chattels and goods through the trespass or forfeiture of their servants, if found in the hands of those servants or deposited anywhere by them, provided they can prove that they own them. And also if any of the Burgesses and aforesaid men shall die, testate or intestate, neither We nor our heirs will cause their goods to be confiscated, but their heirs shall have them wholly, provided it is shown that the chattels belonged to the deceased and the heirs give sufficient notice and pledge. Wherefore we wish and firmly command, for Ourselves and our heirs, that the aforesaid Burgesses and honest men of Monmouth and their heirs, shall have for ever the liberties and immunities here set out. And we forbid, on forfeiture of ten pounds to Us, that any one should presume to annoy or trouble them in connection with any of the said liberties and immunities.

In Witness

The Venerable Father Peter, bishop of Hereford

Humfrey de Bohun, earl of Hereford and Essex

John de Plessy, earl of Warwick

Robert Walerand

Walter de Clifford

William de Stuteville

Roger de Clifford

Walkelin de Ardern

Ralph de Bakepuz

William, Gernun and others.

Given by our hand at Hereford on the third day of August in the 40th year of our Reign.

(P.R.O., C 146/9843)

APPENDIX F

THE TRADE OF THE TOWN, 1296-7

THE King to the Bailiffs and honest men of Monmouth, greeting; Know that at the instance of Henry of Lancaster, our well beloved nephew and your lord, we have granted to you, in aid of the enclosing of the aforesaid town, and for the greater security of these parts, that from the day of completion of these present to the end of five years fully completed you may levy in the said town,

on every quarter of corn for sale	1 obol
on every horse, mare and cow for sale	1 ob.
on every hide of horse, mare, ox and cow, freshly salted or tanned for sale	1 farthing
on every cart carrying fresh or salted meat for sale	3 ob.
on five fat hogs for sale	1 ob.
on ten small (pigs)	1 ob.
on every fresh salmon for sale	1 f.
on every lamprey for sale before Easter	1 f.
on ten sheep, goats or pigs for sale	1 d.
on ten fleeces for sale	1 ob.
on every hundred skins of sheep, goats, stags or deer	1 d.
on every hundred skins of lambs, kids, hares, coneys, foxes, cats and squirrels	1 ob.
on every cartload of salt for sale	1 d.
on every quarter of meal of beans and pease for sale	1 f.
on every horse load of cloth for sale	1 ob.
on every complete piece of cloth for sale	1 ob.
on every hundred of linen yarn or Irish, Welsh or Worsted cloth	1 ob.
on every piece of silk-with-gold, Samite, Diaper or Baudekin	1 ob.
on every piece of silk without gold, mixed with Cendall	1 f.
on every ship coming to the town laden with goods for sale	3 d.
on every horse-load of sea fish	1 ob.
on every cask of wine or cider (?)	3 ob.
on every horse-load of cider	1 ob.
on every horse-load of honey for sale	1 d.
on every cask of honey for sale	3 d.
on every bag of wool	4 d.
on every bushel (?) of cloth (?) brought by cart for sale	2 d.
on every horse-load of cloth or small articles brought to the town for sale	1 ob.
on every cartload of iron for sale	1 d.
on every cartload of lead for sale	2 d.

on every horse-load of tan for sale	1 d.
on every pot of pitch or grease (?) for sale	1 d.
on every hundred of Alum and copper (?)	1 d.
on every two thousand of faggots (?) for sale	1 f.
on every horse-load of garlic	1 ob.
on every thousand herrings	1 f.
on every hundred planks (?) for sale	1 ob.
on every millstone	1 ob.
on every pot of cheese and butter for sale	1 ob.
on every dozen horse-loads of charcoal	1 ob.
on every cartload of firewood	1 ob.
on every horse-load of firewood	1 f.
on every thousand nails for the roofs of houses	1 f.
on every hundred horse shoes, iron nails and cart nails	1 ob.
on every two thousand nails other than those above	1 f.
on every horse-load of miscellaneous goods coming to the town and valued at more than two shillings	1 f.
on every hundred of tin, brass and copper	2 d.
on every hundred of Spanish steel	1 ob.
on every ship laden with turf, chalk or stone	2 d.
on every hundred Aberdeen fish (?)	1 d.
on every hundred stockfish	1 ob.
on every 10 stone of hemp (?) (petris canabi)	1 f.
on every ten gallons of oil	1 f.
on every vat and lead cooling trough for brewing	1 ob.
on every hundred salmon, mullet, congers and dozen salted eels	1 d.

and therefore we command you to levy the above customs to the end of the time appointed, but at the end of that time, the practice is to cease and be abolished.

In witness of which, to last for five years, the King himself, before he crossed the narrow sea.

(P.R.O., C 66/117).

The charter was translated by E.H. Culley in Papers on Monmouth, *etc. read at the meeting of the Bristol and Gloucestershire Archaeological Society in Monmouth in 1896. Mr. Culley's translation has been adopted with slight modifications here. For a more recent version see M.L.J. Rowlands,* Monnow Bridge and Gate, *Alan Sutton, 1994. The charter was renewed by Edward II in 1315 for three years.*

BILL OF FARE FOR THE MAYOR OF MONMOUTH'S DINNER,

(Mr. Silas Blandford, October 4th, 1773.)

	£.	s.	d.
15 Couple Ducks	1	8	0
2 Necks Pork	0	15	0
8 Rumps and 3 Ribs Beef	4	12	9
8 Hams	3	16	0
23 Couples Fowls, 1s. 4d.	1	10	8
8 Turkies	1	1	0
16 Pigeons	0	6	0
2 Loins Veal	1	0	0
Mutton for Pasties	0	2	6
Veal for Stuffing ye Turkies	0	2	6
Flour for Puddings and Pastry	0	12	0
5 Puddings for ye dinner and 3 to have cold	1	2	0
Brandy for the Puddings	0	0	6
8lb. Suet for the Puddings	0	2	8
40lb. Butter, at 8d.	1	6	8
4 dishes Scotch Collops	0	7	0
Grocery	0	19	9
Baking the Pastries	0	5	0
Dressing the Dinner	3	3	0
3 Women's Hire	0	4	0
Gave the Cook	0	5	0
Servants	0	5	0
18lb. Bacon	0	12	0
Bread	1	7	0
Mustard	0	0	6
112 gallons Ale, at 1s. per gallon	5	12	0
12 Tongues	0	18	0
9 Apple Pies	0	18	0
6 Damson Pies	0	12	0
10 doz. Cheese Cakes and Tarts	0	15	0
6 Geese	0	18	0
	£34	19	6

In addition to this regal fare, we find (as was then the annual custom in this town), substantial presents from the guests, such as the Duke of Beaufort, 2 fat Bucks; 3 brace of Carp and 1 of Tench, Mr. Hughes, Treaddam; Flat fish from Sir John Stepney; 14 bottles old Jamaica Rum, distilled in ye year 1750, to fill the 'Kemey's Bowl,' from Mr. Gardner, Kemeys Bartholey; Wine, Spirits, Game, and other rare delicacies from various individuals innumerable.

To compare prices The Monmouthshire Gazette *printed the cost of the Mayor of* Norwich's *dinner in 1561. This was a much grander affair with the Duke and Duchess of Norfolk as guests.*

	£.	s.	d.
Eight stone of beef, at 8d. a stone, and a sirloin	0	5	8
Two collars of brawn	0	1	0
Four cheeses, at 4d. a cheese	0	1	4
Eight pints of butter	0	1	6
A hinder quarter of veal	0	0	10
A leg of mutton	0	0	5
A fore quarter of veal	0	0	5
Loin of mutton and shoulder of veal	0	0	9
Breast and coat of mutton	0	0	7
Six pullets	0	1	0
Four couple of rabbits	0	1	8
Four brace of partridges	0	2	0
Two Guinea cocks	0	1	6
Two couple of mallard	0	1	0
Thirty-four eggs	0	0	6
Bushel of flour	0	0	6
Peck of oatmeal	0	0	2
Sixteen white bread loves	0	0	4
Eighteen loaves of white wheat-bread	0	0	9
Three loaves of meslin bread	0	0	8
Nutmegs, mace, cinnamon, and cloves	0	0	3
Four pounds of Barbary sugar	0	1	0
Sixteen oranges	0	0	2
A barrel of double strong beer	0	2	6
A barrel of table beer	0	1	0
A quarter of wood	0	2	2
Two gallons of white wine and Canary	0	2	0
Fruit, almonds, sweet water, perfumes	0	0	4
The cook's wages	0	1	2
	£1	12	9

GLOSSARY

ADVOWSON	patronage of a church
ALMERY	cupboard for books
APPORT	revenue
AVERAGIUM	Welsh hauling service
BARDED	armoured
BARTON	home farm or barn of the demesne
BAUDEKYN	rich fabric interwoven with gold thread
BRATTICES	breastwork or parapet
BURGAGE	land held of the lord at an annual rent
BURGESS	occupant of a burgage with freedom to trade within the town on payment of an annual charge of 12d
CARREL	an enclosure for study
CARUCATE	ploughland, usually c120 acres
CASTLE COWLES	payment to the lord of 17 gallons of ale from every brew for sale
CHARGER	large dish
CHENCE MONEY	an annual payment for permission to trade
COMMOTE	a community, a Welsh division of a lordship
COMORTHA	alms, gifts
CORRODY	an annual payment for life
COTTAR	peasant
COVER	Welsh cyfar, a ploughing measure. In Monmouth 3 covers equalled 2 acres
CROWDER	a Welsh stringed instrument
CUSTOMARY TENANT	one bound to the lord by ancient customs
DEODAND	a gift to God, the cause of injury
DEMESNE	arable land belonging to the lord
ESCHEATOR	agent ensuring land reverts to the lord when a tenant dies
FALCHION	a broad sword with curved end
FEE FARM	an annual payment to the lord replacing several individual dues and charges
FOREIGNRY	the Welshry
FORESTAGE	a duty paid to the king's foresters
FORESTALLING	buying or taking goods on their way to market
GARDEROBE	a wardrobe or lavatory
GLAIVE	a blade on a long handle
GRANGE	the granary of the lordship
GWESTFA	feast dues paid to the lord by the community
HUNDRED	a subdivision of the shire with its own courts
JUSTICIAR	chief political and judicial officer
KILTH	Welsh cylch, a payment for the circuit courts

153

LEIR	a fine for adultery and incontinence, paid by the girl's father
LITURGICAL KALENDAR	a set of rules for public worship
LOLLARDS	heretics holding the views of Wycliffe
LORDSHIP	the estate lands of a lord
MACHICOLIS	parapets with holes through which missiles were dropped
MARK	13s 4d, two-thirds of £1
MERCHIET	payment to the lord by a tenant on the marriage of a daughter
MESLIN	mixed grain, especially rye and wheat
OBOL	half a penny
ORIEL	a projecting window in an upper storey; usually fifteenth or sixteenth century
PANNAGE	payment to allow swine to feed in the lord's wood
PATRIA	the Welsh lands of the lordship
PICCAGE	rent paid for ground on which to set up a stall at a fair or market
PLEAD	to present a case in court
PLOUGH	land that can be cultivated by one plough
PONTAGE	toll exacted for the use of a bridge
PORTCULLIS	a defensive gate raised in grooves
PRISE	an exaction, a toll
PROCURATIONS	provision of entertainment for bishops, etc.
RECTOR	one responsible for maintaining the chancel of a church and the recipient of the great tithes
RECUSANCY	refusal to attend the services of the church of England
REGRATING	buying goods from a market to sell at a profit
REGULAR	one belonging to a religious or monastic order
SESTER	from Latin *sextarium*, a measure both liquid and dry; for honey it is reckoned at 32 ounces
SLATTERS	slates
SMOKESILVER	payment for the right to gather firewood
SUITORS	attenders at court
SYNODALS	payments to church councils
TAK	payment for compulsory feeding of swine in the lord's wood
TALLAGE	payment levied on bondsmen by the lord
VICAR	a priest charged with the care of the nave of a church and its congregation; the recipient of the lesser tithes
WELSHRY	the Patria, Welsh lands in the lordship
WOODHENS	Hens paid to the lord in return for the right to gather firewood

BIBLIOGRAPHY

(Abbreviations for some of the more frequently cited sources appear on page 8)

Ashby, George.	*Poems*. Bateson, ed., Early English Text Society.
Bagnall-Oakeley, M. E.	'The Fortifications of Monmouth' (MCAA, 1896).
Baldwin, J. F.	'The Chancery of the Duchy of Lancaster', (BHR IV, 12, 1927).
Birch, W. de Gray	*Memorials of the See and Cathedral of Llandaff*, 1912.
Bold, W. E.	*Methodism and its Beginnings in Monmouth*, Monmouth, 1974.
Bradney, J. A.	*A History of Monmouthshire*, vol. I, 1904.
Buckland, Kirstie	'The Monmouth Cap', in *Costume*, vol.13, 1979.
	'The Skenfrith Cope and its Companions', in *Textile History*, 14(2), 125-139, 1983.
Charles, B.G.	*The Welsh, their language and placenames in Archenfield and Oswestry*, Cardiff, 1963.
Clarke, Basil, ed.	Geoffrey of Monmouth: *Vita Merlini*, CUP.
Clarke, S.	'The Origins of Medieval Pottery in South East Wales'. (*Medieval Ceramics*, 1991).
	'Evidence for a Pre-Norman Structure at Monmouth', (*Monmouthshire Antiquary*, XII, 19)
	'Archaeological Evidence for Cooking without Fire'. (*Medieval and Later Pottery in Wales*, II, 1989).
Coates, S. D.	*The Water Powered Industries of the Lower Wye Valley*, Monmouth Museum, 1992.
	Water Mills of the Monnow, Trothy and Upper Wye Valley, 2 vols., 1978, 1983.
Davies, Canon E. T.	*An Ecclesiastical History of Monmouthshire*, pt.1, 1953.
Davies, R. R.	*Lordship and Society in the March of Wales, 1282-1400*, Oxford, 1978.
	The Revolt of Owain Glyn Dwr, Oxford, 1995.
Davies, Wendy	*An Early Welsh Microcosm*, London, 1978.
Dreghorn, W.	*Geology Explained in the Forest of Dean and Wye Valley*, 1968.
Fowler, Kenneth	*The King's Lieutenant*, 1968.
Graham, Rose	'Four Alien Priories in Monmouthshire', (*Journal of British Arch. Assoc.*, 1929).
Griffinhoofe, H. G.	'The Mediaeval Tiles in St. Mary's Church, Monmouth', Monmouth, 1984.
Griffiths, R. A.	*The Principality of Wales in the Later Middle Ages, 1277-1536*, Cardiff, 1972.
Halliday, G. F.	*Llandaff Church Plate*, London, 1901.
Harris, G. L., ed.	*Henry V: The Practice of Kingship*, OUP, 1985.
Harris, Rev. S.M.	'The Kalendar of the Vitae Sanctorum Wallensium (Vespasian A xiv)' in JHSCW, III, 8.
Heath, Charles	*Historical and Descriptive Account of the Ancient and Present State of the town of Monmouth*, 1804.
Hopson, Mary	*A Record of the Memorial Stones in Monmouth Parish Churchyard*, 1988.
Howell, R.	*A History of Gwent*, Gomer, 1988.
Jenkyns, Rhys	'Iron-making in the Forest of Dean'. (*Transactions of Newcomen Society*, 1925/6).
Kissack, K. E.	*Mediaeval Monmouth*, Newport, 1974.
	Monmouth: The Making of a County Town, Phillimore, 1975.

	'Religious Life in Monmouth, 1066-1536'. (JHSCW, vol. XIV, 1964).
Knowles, C. H.	'Henry V and the Historians', (PM, no. 21, 1946).
Lane, M.P.	'The Barton, Monmouth', *Monmouthshire Beacon*, 1946.
Marchegay, Paul	'Les Prieurés Anglais de St. Florent près Saumur'. In *Bibliothéque de l'Ecole des Chartes*, 1879.
	'Chartes Normandes de l'Abbaye de St. Florent', 1880. There is a microfilm of most of the charters in the MBA and some are calendared by J. H. Round (q.v.).
Matthews, J. Hobson	*Monmouth Records*, 1908. In Mss amongst MBA.
	'Old Monmouth', (*Archaeologia Cambrensis*, 1908).
Morgan, Octavius	'The Ancient Seal of the Monmouth Chancery', (Proceedings of Society of Antiquaries, no. 4).
Padel, O. J.	'Geoffrey of Monmouth and Cornwall', (*Cambridge Medieval Celtic Studies*, no. 8, Winter 1984).
Potter, Rev. P.	'St. Thomas, Overmonnow', (*Archaeologia Cambrensis*, 1886).
Powell, D. A.	*St. Mary's Catholic Church, Monmouth, 1793-1993*, 1993.
Pugh, F. H.	'Monmouth Recusants in the reigns of Elizabeth and James I'. (SWMRS, IV).
Rees, William	*South Wales and the March, 1284-1415*, OUP, 1924.
	(With A. J. Roderick), 'Ministers Accounts for the Lordships of Monmouth and Three Castles', (SWMRS, I, II, III, IV).
Renn, D. F.	'The Anglo-Norman Keep', (*Journal of British Archaeological Association*, XXIII, 1960).
Round, J. H.	*Calender of Documents Preserved in France, 918-1206*, H.M.S.O. 1899.
	Studies in Peerage and Family History, 1901.
Rowlands, M. L. J	*Monnow Bridge and Gate*, Alan Sutton 1994.
Searle, E.	*The Rivers of Monmouthshire*, Davies, 1970.
Seaton, Rev. Preb.	*A History of Archenfield*, Hereford, 1903.
Sockett, A. L.	*Monmouth District in Antiquity*, Monmouth, 1960.
Somerville, R.	*The Duchy of Lancaster I, 1265-1603*, London, 1954.
Taylor, A. J.	*Monmouth Castle and Great Castle House*, HMSO, 1976.
Tucker, Clifford	'The Parliamentary Representation of the Monmouth District Constituency', (PM, 18 & 20, 1965).
Vaillant, Mme. A.	*La Marveilleuse Vie de St. Florent*, Poitiers, 1964.
Wakeman, Thomas.	'On the Priory of Monmouth', 1862; 'On the Chancery of Monmouth', 1858; 'The Tiles of Monmouth Priory', 1868, in *Monmouthshire and Caerleon Antiquarian Association Papers*.
Walker, David.	'Hereford and the Laws of Breteuil'. (Woolhope Transactions, XL, 1970, pt. 1).
Warlow, W. M.	*A History of the Charities of William Jones*, Bristol, 1899.
Watkins, M. P.	'The Lordship of Monmouth and the Herefordshire Monmouthshire Border'. (Woolhope Transactions, XXXVII, 1961).
Watson, Graham	*Militiamen and Sappers, a History of the Royal Monmouthshire Royal Engineers (Militia), 1996.*
Williams, D. H.	'Monmouth Priory at the Suppression, 1534-37'. (*Monmouthshire Antiquary*, III, pts. 3 & 4).
	'Medieval Monasticism in Monmouthshire'. (Ibid., vol. X., 1994).
	'Grace Dieu Abbey'. (Ibid., I, Pt.??, 1964).
Wood, J. G.	*The Lordship, Castle and Town of Chepstow*, 1910.
Wright, Arthur	*The Church Bells of Monmouthshire*, 1942.

INDEX

159